Table of Contents

Introduction

There are many great musicians who don't know how to read music. They usually learn "by ear," which means the ability to listen to music and imitate it. (This is of course an important skill for musicians to have – after all, music is all about listening.) If you have learned this way, you may feel that the first few chapters in this book are bringing you back to basics. You may also feel that learning the technical aspects of music will diminish your musicianship. My own observations of students tell me otherwise. I have found that the more you learn about music, the better player you become. Everything about music is interconnected, and increasing your technical knowledge can only improve all aspects of your musicianship.

The purpose of this series is to intertwine different aspects of music – theory, technical, aural, history, appreciation, and more – in a way that encourages you to develop an intrinsic understanding of music. At times it may be difficult, but in the end I hope you come to appreciate and understand the value of what music has to offer.

Ultimately, of course, it's not what you learn in this book that matters – it's how you use it in your own life. For every student, this will be different. But part of what makes music so important is that everyone has a unique relationship with it. Take what you learn here and embrace it, making it your own to share with the world.

Unit 1

"*Music expresses that which cannot be said
and on which it is impossible to be silent.*"

~ Victor Hugo

Unit 1

One of the primary reasons we learn to write music is communication. If you are a writer, for instance, you have a story to tell. One way to tell that story is by verbally explaining everything that happens. But imagine you are telling the story and someone walks in during the middle and you have to start over. Or you want to tell your story to someone in another country. Or if you're really ambitious, you might want millions of people to enjoy your story. Trying to talk to a million people at different times might make you pretty tired, so instead you could write your story down on paper, send an email, start a blog, or publish a book. Writing words gives you the freedom to communicate to more people in a more efficient, concise way.

The same principle applies to music. Notes on a page are simply ways to communicate your musical story to more people. Knowing how to write music gives you the ability to pass music on to others. Knowing how to read music gives you the ability to play what other musicians have written.

I've made the comparison above to literature because music is very similar to language (in fact, music has been called the "universal language"). And just like learning a new tongue, you must first start with the basics before reading or writing entire novels. In this chapter, we will start with the essential building blocks of music: notes on a staff.

1.1 Theory

Notation

You've probably seen a sheet of music before, with symbols, shapes, numbers, lines, and foreign languages. Seeing this for the first time can sometimes be overwhelming, but once you learn what everything means it is actually very easy. What's more, most musical notation is consistent across different genres, styles, and countries, making it easy to communicate sounds to many different people regardless of what language they speak.

Music is written on a **staff**. A staff is a set of five lines and four spaces that looks like this:

When looking at the staff, the lines and spaces are counted from the bottom up. The lowest line is "Line 1" and the highest line is "Line 5." Likewise, the lowest space is "Space 1" and the highest space is "Space 4."

The symbols that are placed on a staff are called **notes**. Notes come in a variety of shapes and sizes. For now, don't worry about what each one means – we'll get to that later in this chapter.

The notes are actually symbols that represent sounds. We call these **pitches.** Notes that are written high on the staff represent higher pitches, and notes written lower on the staff represent lower pitches. "High" and "low" refer the sounds themselves (not how far a pitch is off the ground!). For reference, take a look at a piano. High pitches are found on the right side of a keyboard, and low pitches are found on the left side of the keyboard.

Treble Clef

Music notes are named after the first seven letters of the alphabet:

A B C D E F G

Once you get to G, you start over again. These seven letters repeat themselves over and over, so as you learn more you will find that many pitches have the same name. Knowing which lines and spaces represent which letters has something to do with another symbol you find on a staff: the **clef**. There are many different kinds of clefs:

For our purposes, we'll be focusing on the first two you see above because they are the most common. The first one is called the **treble clef**. The treble clef is also known as the **G clef** because the curl wraps around the note G.

Notice that the curl wraps around the second line of the clef, so you know that pitch is G. From there, you can use what you already know of the musical alphabet to find the other notes: The space just above G would be A, the next line would be B, the next space C, and so on.

E   F   G   A   B   C   D   E   F

However, there is an easier way to remember the lines and spaces. To memorize the lines, remember **Every Good Boy Does Fine.**

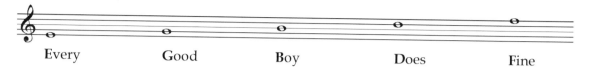

To learn the spaces, you can remember that they spell the word FACE.

"Treble" is a word that refers to high sounds, so notes that you see on a treble clef represent higher pitches. We'll be exploring more about that later this chapter.

Bass Clef

The second clef we'll be concerned with is called the **bass clef.** The bass clef is also known as the **F clef** because the note F is found between the two dots.

As before, if you know where the note F is, you can easily deduce where the other notes are:

However, there is of course an easier way to learn the notes. To remember the notes, I like to think of one of favorite foods: **Good Burritos Don't Fall Apart.**

The lines can be remembered with **All Cows Eat Grass.**

The word "Bass" refers to low sounds (think of a bass guitar or a bass singer), so notes on the bass clef will represent lower pitches. Working together, the bass and treble clefs cover many notes of our musical language.

Ledger Lines

The treble and bass staffs cover many notes, but if you look at a piano you will see that there are many more than just 18 keys to play. (Theoretically, the pitches could continue practically forever above and below the notes on the keyboard – we just might not be able to hear them!) To write notes that aren't found on the treble or bass clefs, we use **ledger lines**. Ledger lines simply extend the staff temporarily so we can write the notes we need.

Notes written with ledger lines simply follow the same alphabetical pattern as the lines and spaces on the staff. Since the top line of the treble staff is F, the space just above is G, the next line A, the next space B, and so on. The same principle applies below the staffs. Take a look at following notes above and below the treble and bass staffs:

Become as familiar as you can with the notes that you've just learned in this unit. Just as you first learn letters before forming words, this musical alphabet will serve as the foundation of bigger and better ideas to come.

1.2 Rhythm

In part one of this unit, you learned how to read musical notes written on a staff. Now that you know *what* notes to play, however, there is something else you need to learn: how *long (or short)* you play each note. This part of music is called **rhythm**, and it's a central part of music as we know it.

Rhythm is a powerful thing - a good groove can make you dance, or a percussion solo can really grab your ears and make you pay attention. Rhythm is, in fact, one of the most essential parts of human life. Not only do we often react to rhythms involuntarily, our own bodies even have a rhythm of their own. Our heartbeat, the way we walk, the blinking of our eyes - all of these create the flow of life we experience. We are all quite literally living and breathing music instruments.

This unit introduces the basic concepts of rhythm. We'll start off by talking about basic rhythmic values and how to organize them on the staff.

Note Values

You may have noticed in the previous section that there were many different kinds of note shapes. The way a note is drawn tells you how long the note is held, or the **duration** of the note.

A **whole note** is a simple oval shape:

Typically a whole note is equal to 4 counts. A **half note** is equal to 2 counts, or ½ the duration of a whole note. It looks like an oval with a stem:

Finally, a **quarter note** is equal to 1 count, or ¼ of a whole note. It looks like a black oval with a stem:

Mathematically, our note values look like this so far:

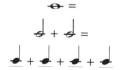

I've said before that musical notation is similar to a language, but the above is a simple example of why music is often said to be mathematical.

One more thing: When notes have stems, it's important to write them in the correct direction. The general guideline is that if the note is written *on or above* the 3rd line, the stems should be drawn downward. If the note is written *below* the 3rd line, stems should be written upward.

The reason for this is to simply keep things organized, however, there are many exceptions to the rule. Often music, especially piano and guitar music, will break this rule for the very reason it's there in the first place – to keep things organized.

Measures

Another organizational tool that is very important in music is the **measure**. A staff is divided into sections by **measure lines**, and the spaces between the lines are called measures.

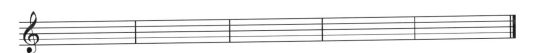

Measures are also referred to as **bars**, and measure lines can be referred to as **bar lines**. Notice the last line above is not only doubled, but is also thicker. This is called a **double bar line** and it indicates that you have reached the end of the music.

Time Signatures

If you look at a piece of music, you will probably immediately notice one more thing that we haven't talked about: the **time signature**. The time signature is a group of two numbers, one stacked on top of the other.

$$\begin{matrix} 9 \\ \vdots \end{matrix} \begin{matrix} 4 \\ 4 \end{matrix}$$

The top number in a time signature tells you how many counts are in each measure. Since the top number in the above example is 4, you would count to 4 then start over.

1 2 3 4   1 2 3 4   Etc.

11

What exactly are you counting? That has to do with the bottom number. Think of this number as being a code. 4 = quarter note, so in the above example you are allowed to have four quarter notes in each measure.

1 2 3 4   1 2 3 4   Etc.

However, it doesn't have to be *literally* four quarter notes – if that was the case, music would get boring very quickly. As long as it adds up to four, you're fine. This is where the musical math is going to come into play again:

1 2 3 4   1 2 3 4   1 2 3 4   1 2 3 4   1 2 3 4

Notice that in the above example, every measure adds up to 4 in some way. Again, it's because the time signature tells you "4 counts" and "4 quarter notes." In your workbook, you'll find several more exercises to help you become acquainted with this material.

Are there different kinds of time signatures? Absolutely! We'll be coming back to this topic several times throughout the book.

1.3 Keyboard Skills

If you're completely new to music, don't be frightened by the topic above – I won't be expecting you to become a concert pianist overnight! When learning about music, however, it helps to have a visual reference (as well as something to make sounds on so you can hear what we're talking about). The piano keyboard is great for this because all the keys are laid out in a very visually compelling way. For a beginner, trying to discuss the theoretical aspects of music on any other instrument would be nearly impossible because it's not as easy to see the notes visually.

As you're learning the material in this book, use the piano as a reference – you'll find that it makes things much easier. To get you started, let's learn about the basic layout of the keyboard.

Middle C

If you take a look at the piano keyboard, you'll notice that there is a pattern: There is a set of two black keys grouped together, followed by a set of three black keys, which is then followed by two, then three, etc. This pattern continues all the way up and down the keyboard.

The white key to the immediate left of the set of two is always C. If you know that this is C, then you can easily find the other notes – the next white key is D, the next E, etc. (We'll discuss the black keys later).

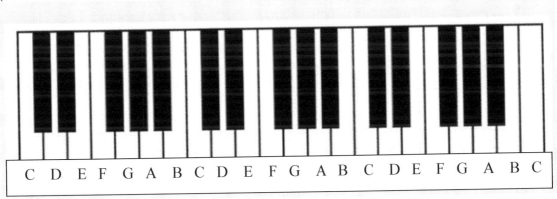

As you can see, the notes on the keyboard repeat themselves over and over. So how do you know which note on the staff represents which key on the piano? As a reference, you can find *middle C*. **Middle C** is quite literally in the middle of the keyboard – on most pianos, it's the C that is closest to the logo.

Piano Notation

On the treble clef, middle C is located just below the staff:

If you know where middle C is, then you can easily find the other notes. The space just above is D – or the next white key, as you just learned – and the space just below is B (the previous white key). Try playing these notes on the piano:

The piano is unique to most other instruments because you read music on both the treble and bass clefs. On the bass clef, you can also use middle C as a reference point:

As before, if you know where middle C is, then you can find the other notes as well. Try playing these notes on the piano:

If you are paying attention, you'll notice that you just played the same notes as before. This can be a confusing concept if you're new to piano, but yes – the same notes can be written on different clefs.

Since piano music is written on both clefs, the staffs are combined to create a **grand staff**. A grand staff looks like this:

Using a grand staff, it's easy to write music that utilizes the entire range of the piano, from low (bass) to high (treble).

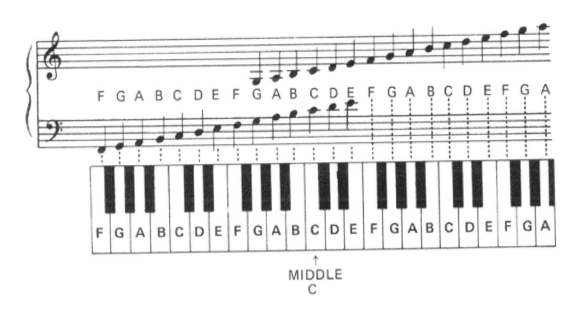

Start getting used to these notes by looking at the exercises in your workbook.

1.4 Aural Skills

Aural skills include topics that are also known as "ear training" and "sight singing." With aural training, there are essentially two goals: 1) to train yourself to recognize music sounds and structures by ear and 2) to be able look at notes written on paper and hear in your head how it's going to sound.

If this scares you, don't throw the book away yet – we're going to take it one step at a time. To make learning this material more effective, most of the work in this aural skills section of each unit will be used in conjunction with the material found online (or CD/mp3s).

Remember as you work through this material that music is first and foremost an aural skill. Music isn't something you can see, touch, smell, or taste – it's something you listen to. Since you probably listen to music many times throughout the day, the work we do in this book is simply refining a skill that you already frequently use.

High and Low Notes

The exercises in this unit will focus on identifying high notes and low notes. You will listen to a series of pitches, then you will choose the one that is higher (or lower) as asked. If you are using the workbook, there are a series of examples already written out for you. Sometimes there will be two pitches to choose from, sometimes more. Sometimes the notes will be played slowly, other times quickly. To practice this material on your own, sit at an instrument such as the piano and play the different pitches. Try to get used to hearing the various sounds that musical instruments can make.

1.5 Music Appreciation

Music hasn't always been written on the five-line staff that we use today. The earliest musical notation consisted of rudimentary shapes, symbols, and sometimes colors. In the Middle Ages, for example, monks developed a system of **neumes** that consisted of shapes and strokes written above the text of a chant. In other countries and cultures, such as Iraq, Persia, and Ancient Greece, scholars invented similar organizational schemes.

These early notational devices often lacked specificity – exact pitches were not notated and it was difficult to determine how long to hold a note. Eventually composers began to write lines to indicate pitch, which soon led to the five-line staff that we have today. Over the course of several hundred years, this system has been refined to allow almost infinite possibilities, and it is possible to indicate virtually all music using the system we have now.

Not that that's kept composers happy, mind you. Innovative musicians are constantly creating new ways to write down sounds. In the 20th century, composers such as George Crumb, John Cage, and John Zorn frequently used **graphic notation** to explain the unusual techniques their music required. This music is very fun to look at, as the colors and symbols blend to create music scores that could be considered works of visual art. And if you listen to their music, you can understand why a new way to write music would be required. The notation is as innovative as their musical ideas.

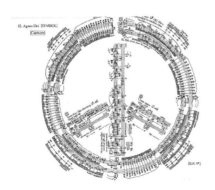

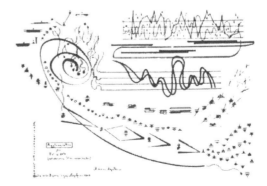

1.6 Research and Discussion

In Unit 1 we spent a lot of time discussing high and low sounds and how they relate to clefs. Although most instruments have quite a wide range of notes, they are typically categorized into one area or another. Instruments that usually play high notes include the flute, violin, piccolo, and soprano and tenor voices. Instruments that usually play low notes include the bass, cello, bassoon, tuba, and alto and bass voices. Two instruments that have a unique range encompassing both high and low notes are the piano and the harp.

Things to think about and discuss:

- What other instruments excel at high notes? Low notes?

- Most music you listen to probably utilizes both high and low notes, but can you find music that features one or the other more prominently?

- Invent a musical instrument using "found objects." Find things around the house that make sound and put them together. *Hint: Percussion instruments can be made out of almost anything.*

1.7 Vocabulary

The following words pertaining to music were used in this unit. Look back through the chapter to find definitions and to make sure you understand them. An excellent online dictionary can be found at: http://www.music.vt.edu/musicdictionary

Staff

Note

Pitch

Clef

Treble Clef

G Clef

Bass Clef

F Clef

Ledger Line

Rhythm

Whole Note

Half Note

Quarter Note

Measure

Measure Line

Time Signature

Middle C

Grand Staff

Neumes

Graphic Notation

Unit 2

*"After silence, that which comes nearest
to expressing the inexpressible is music."*

~ Aldous Huxley

Unit 2

In Unit 1, you learned what notes to play and how long to hold them. While those are the basics of notation, the actual music doesn't happen until the performer plays the instrument. This unit is about *how* to play the music.

Take a single note – choose any one you like – and play it. You might decide to play it long or short, loud or soft, fast or slow. This is where it gets interesting, because there are infinite ways to play the same note. If there are 10 people in the same room, each one could play a completely different way. And we're only talking about one note. With each pitch you add, you compound the equation. With such variety and selection, one can see how it's possible to constantly create new, original music.

2.1 Theory

Dynamics

One choice you can make when performing music is how loud or soft to play. **Dynamics** and **dynamic signs** designate volume. The two basic dynamics are loud and soft, but in music we use the Italian terms **forte** and **piano**. Instead of writing the entire words, however, in music score they are usually indicated by the symbols below.

Forte $\boldsymbol{f}$
Piano $\boldsymbol{p}$

Loud and soft doesn't cover enough ground, of course, so we also have ways to indicate more subtle gradations of volume. You can use "moderately loud" and "moderately soft." As before, we turn to the Italians for their vocabulary. **Mezzo** means moderately, so we have **mezzo forte** and **mezzo piano**.

Mezzo Forte $\boldsymbol{mf}$
Mezzo Piano $\boldsymbol{mp}$

Perhaps you also want to play "very loud" or "very soft." Adding **issimo** to a word means very.

Fortissimo $\boldsymbol{ff}$
Pianissimo $\boldsymbol{pp}$

From soft to loud, the dynamic signs would go in this order:

$$pp - p - mp - mf - f - ff$$

If you play them this way, gradually soft to loud, it is called a **crescendo**. The opposite is called a **decrescendo** or **diminuendo**. These gestures are often indicated with the symbols below.

crescendo or *cresc.* (gradually louder)

decrescendo or *decresc.* (gradually softer)
diminuendo or *dim.*

Tempo

In addition to playing music at different volumes, you can also play it at different speeds, or **tempos**. As with dynamics, most tempos are also written in Italian. Here are some tempo markings you can use:

Grave — slow and solemn
Lento — very slow
Lento Moderato — moderately slow
Largo — very slow, like *lento*
Adagio — slow and stately
Andante — at a walking pace
Andante Moderato — a bit faster than *andante*
Moderato — moderately
Allegro — fast and bright or "cheerfully"
Allegro moderato — moderately quick
Vivace — lively and fast
Presto — very fast

When we learned dynamics, we learned that there could be a gradual change in volume. The same applies for tempos. In some parts of music, you may not want to keep a steady pace – you might want to speed up or slow down. In that case, you could use the following terms:

accelerando or *accel.* — gradually faster
ritardando or *rit.* — gradually slower

Tempo markings have been used since the Baroque Era (1600-1750), but, as you might guess, tempos can be very subjective. One person's "walking pace" (**adagio**), for example, might qualify as another's **vivace**. In the early 19th century, an invention called the **metronome** made it easier for composers to specify the exact tempo they wanted something played at. Metronome markings are measured in "beats per minute," or "bpm." At a tempo marking of 70 bpm, for example, the metronome will click 70 times during the course of a minute.

Beethoven was one of the first composers to use a metronome, but since some of his markings are a little contradictory, many people question if his device was in proper working order. Nowadays, most metronomes are digital (you can even find them on the internet), guaranteeing accuracy.

Articulations

In addition to dynamics (volume) and tempo (speed), the notes themselves can be played in different ways. For example, read the following sentence: He gave her a necklace. Depending on what you were trying to emphasize, you might say it in one of the following ways:

HE gave her a necklace.
He GAVE her a necklace!
He gave HER a necklace?
He gave her a NECKLACE...

Just as the emphasized word and varying punctuation gives the same sentence completely different meanings, emphasizing different notes (or the same note in a different way) can change the meaning of a musical phrase. The way a note is played is referred to as **articulation**. Some examples, along with the symbols that represent them, are below:

staccato – play short and detached –

accent – play the note louder, with emphasis –

tenuto – hold the note for its full value –

fermata – hold the note longer that its normal duration –

2.2 Rhythm

We have already learned three note values as well as how a time signature works. This doesn't seem like much, but it actually allows us to write and understand quite a bit of music. If you start listening to music carefully and looking at music scores, you'll find a plethora of examples of all of these concepts. There is, however, much more to learn.

The Dotted Half Note

You know the note values for 4 counts, 2 counts, and 1 count (the whole, half, and quarter notes, respectively). What about 3? The note value for 3 counts looks like a half note with a dot.

It is, in fact, referred to as a **dotted half note**. Now time for more of the musical math we discussed before: The dot doesn't actually mean "3," it's a symbol that means something specific. Whenever a dot follows a note, it increases its value by ½. Therefore, a dotted half note is actually read like this:

$$\text{(dotted half)} = \underset{\substack{\text{(original}\\ \text{note}\\ \text{value)}}}{} + \underset{\substack{\text{(½ of}\\ \text{original}\\ \text{value)}}}{} = 3$$

You've probably already realized that a dot can be added to any note. We'll be talking more about this concept in later chapters.

Time Signatures

Remember that the two numbers of a time signature mean different things. The top number tells you how many counts are in a measure, the bottom number is a code for what type of note gets a count (4 = quarter note). In the time signature below, there are four quarter notes in a measure.

There are many other time signatures, and as you may suspect, almost any combination is theoretically possible. There are, however, some time signatures that are more common that others. In the time signature below, there are <u>two</u> quarter notes in a measure.

As before, it doesn't mean literally, two quarter notes – as long as the notes in measure add up to two, anything is possible.

Another common time signature is 3/4, meaning <u>three</u> quarter notes in a measure.

Check out the workbook for more examples of these time signatures. There are many other possibilities, of course, but these are two of the most common and most practical. If you really wanted to, you could make something like 64/4… but I'm not sure the person playing the music would like that very much.

2.3 Keyboard Skills

Before the piano was invented, there was an instrument called the harpsichord. This device looked very similar to a piano, but was smaller and not as sturdy. The main difference, however, was the way that it made sound.

When you press a key on a harpsichord, there is a device that plucks, or pulls, the string. There are two consequences of this: First, the sound is very metallic, nasally, and bright. Second, and more importantly, there is no way to control the volume of the instrument. If a pro wrestler slammed his fist on the keyboard as hard as he could, the sound will be the same as if a dainty princess played it in the 17th century.

The invention of the piano was remarkable for one single reason: Instead of plucking a string, when you play a key on a piano a padded hammer *strikes* the string. Because of this, it became instantly possible to piano music at different dynamics.

The original name, in fact, was *clavicembalo col piano e forte*, literally "harpsichord with soft and loud." This was eventually shortened to simply *pianoforte*, indicating that one could play both *piano* (soft) and *forte* (loud). Over time this was yet again abbreviated to the name that we know it as today.

Basic Right Hand Fingerings

To show what fingers to use on certain notes in piano music, fingers are labeled with numbers. On both hands, the thumb is "1," index "2," middle is "3," ring is "4," and pinky is "5."

Using the right hand, place the thumb on Middle C. You'll see that your fingers fall naturally on the keyboard. Try playing five notes in a row, like this:

Now try going up and down like this:

Practice this several times until you feel comfortable.

Basic Left Hand Fingerings

On the left hand, the finger numbers are the same, but because of our indispensable opposable thumbs, the patterns will be a little different. Place the pinky of the left hand on the C below Middle C and try playing this:

As you can see, the pattern of notes you are playing is the same, but the numbers, or fingerings, are different.

Try playing both hands together:

Practice this several times, and also look at the exercises found in the workbook. As you feel comfortable, begin adding in dynamics, tempos, and articulations to add some variety.

2.4 Aural Skills

In the last unit, we discussed hearing high notes and low notes. Another important aspect of ear training is rhythm. The exercises on this unit's workbook page will help you begin to identify rhythms by ear.

In some of the exercises, you will listen to a rhythm and choose which music example is being played. In other exercises, you will hear a rhythm and be asked to write it down or complete the measure. As you listen, counting out loud will help you keep track of where you are. Be sure to pay attention to the differences in whole, half, quarter, and dotted half notes.

2.5 Music Appreciation

Since we have now introduced the idea of different time signatures, you might be questioning why these are necessary. The basic answer is that it has to do with the *feeling* of the music. To understand this concept, listen to a dance. If you hear a **waltz** (which is commonly in 3/4 time), you'll hear a strong pulse on the first beat, then lighter pulses on beats 2 and 3. The result is something like this:

ONE - two - three - ONE - two - three

If you watch people dancing to this, or if you have danced a waltz yourself, you'll see that the movements exactly match the strong and weak pulses. Other dances follow different patterns. A **polka**, for example, is in 2/4, giving a strong "boom – chuck" feeling.

While not all music is a dance, all music does have some relation to the time signature. Military **marches** are usually written in 2/4 so soldiers can keep a quick, strong pace in unified motion. Listen to some of your favorite music and see if you can determine what time signature it is written in.

2.6 Research and Discussion

One of the things I find most fascinating about music is the fact that everyone can play the same music in different ways. A great example of this is when a band or musician performs a cover song. Many of the elements will remain similar to the original – usually enough that you'll be able to recognize the song – but the band will put their own unique spin that makes it sound like "their own." This could be achieved by dynamics, tempos, articulation, even different instrumentation or the whether the singer is male or female. With music, the possibilities are virtually endless.

Things to think about and discuss:

- Find two different versions of the same song and compare them. What makes them similar or different? How do the artists make the same music sound different?

- Choose a new term that you learned this unit (such as a dynamic marking, tempo, or articulation) and find a piece of music that exemplifies it.

- Find music that is in 4/4, 3/4, and 2/4. Why is the music written in that specific time signature? How does the time signature affect the way the music is performed?

2.7 Vocabulary

The following words pertaining to music were used in this unit. Look back through the chapter to find definitions and to make sure you understand them. An excellent online dictionary can be found at: http://www.music.vt.edu/musicdictionary

Dynamics

Forte

Piano

Mezzo

issimo

Crescendo

Decrescendo/ Diminuendo

Tempo

Lento

Largo

Adagio

Andante

Moderato

Allegro

Vivace

Accelerando

Ritardando

Articulation

Dotted Half Note

Waltz

Polka

Unit 3

*"Music should strike fire from the heart of man,
and bring tears from the eyes of woman."*

~ Ludwig Van Beethoven

Unit 3

You may have noticed that we have only been discussing the white keys on the piano. These are known as **natural notes**. The black keys are called **accidentals**. Accidentals aren't mistakes that you make when you're playing – they are the pitches between the natural notes.

3.1 Theory

Sharps

A **sharp** sign placed before a note makes the sound of that pitch higher. On the piano, if a note is accompanied by a "♯" you would play the key to its immediate right.

Find the note C on the keyboard. If you play the black key to its immediate right, that note would be C sharp (C♯).

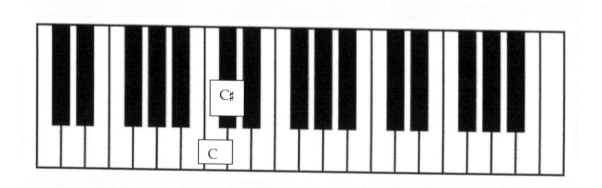

Take note: If you are writing or speaking about notes, the sharp sign (or the word "sharp") comes *after* the letter name. When writing music, however, the sharp sign is placed *before* the note.

Try finding the following notes on the piano:

If a note can be raised, then it can also be lowered. A **flat** sign placed before a note lowers that pitch. Find the note G on the piano. The key to its immediate left is G flat.

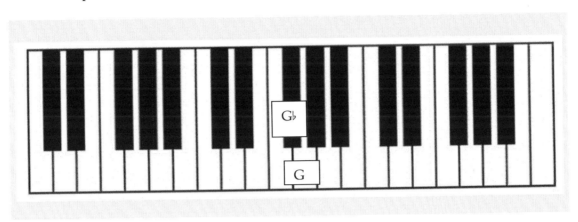

As before, if you are writing or speaking, the word flat (or sign) comes after the letter. In music notation, the flat sign is written before the note.

Find the following notes on the piano:

Naturals

We have been referring to the natural notes as their simple letter names. This is usually how they are spoken of, however, another way to refer to them is as "B natural," "D natural," etc. The **natural** sign looks like this: ♮

Why would you need to use the natural sign? First, let's talk a little more about accidentals. When an accidental is written before a note, it stays in effect for the entire measure. The measure line cancels the accidental.

In the example above, the note on beat 4 of the first measure is B♭ because there is a flat sign before the first B (on beat one). Even though there is no flat sign preceding it, the accidental remains in effect. The note on beat 1 of the second measure, however, is B♮

because the measure line has cancelled the flat sign. To write B♭, as we have on beat four, you must again use the accidental.

Now back to the natural sign. Let's say you would like the note on beat four to be B♮. You would need to use the natural sign in this way:

In this case, the natural sign cancels the flat, making the note on beat four a natural note.

Enharmonic Notes

In our discussion of sharps and flats, you may have noticed something interesting: Sometimes the same note can be called two different names. For example, play the following two notes:

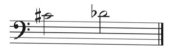

When you play C♯ or D♭, you'll notice that it's the same note on the keyboard:

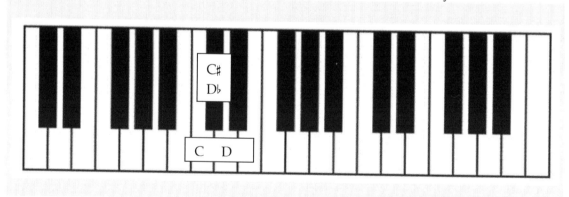

When two notes sound the same but can be written differently, they are called **enharmonic notes**. Try finding these enharmonic pairs:

34

Additional Accidentals

We haven't discussed all of the accidental notes yet. Take a look at the piano keyboard, and you'll notice that there are no black keys between the notes E and F or between B and C. However, this doesn't mean we never use accidentals with them. Remember that a sharp sign indicates you play the key to its immediate right, so the E♯ is enharmonic to the note F. Likewise, F♭ is enharmonic to E.

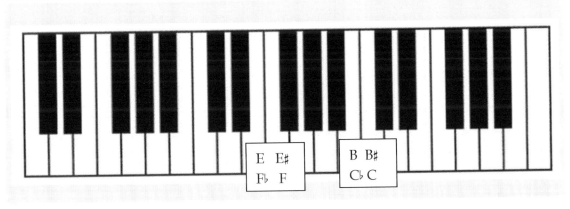

The other pair of notes this applies to is B and C. You may wonder, as many students do, what the point of writing something so confusing would be. At this point it's difficult to explain why and make a convincing argument, so we'll address that later in the book.

3.2 Rhythm

Although counting is the most important part of rhythm, there is a lot more than meets the eye. This unit will explore some of the rhythmic accessories needed in music.

Rests

In conversations, you can't be talking all the time – sometimes you have to give your jaw a break or let someone else say something. In music, there are also times when you will need to stop the sound. The symbols we use to indicate silence are called **rests.**

For most note values, there is a rest equivalent:

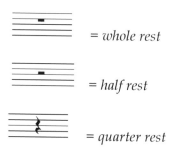

= *whole rest*

= *half rest*

= *quarter rest*

Take careful notice of the difference between the whole rest and the half rest. The look very similar, but the whole rest hangs *below* the fourth line, whereas the half rest sits *above* the third line.

As with note values, we can show this mathematically with the following equation:

36

Ties and Slurs

By using the note values you know so far, you can create quite a variety of rhythms within your music. But what if you need to hold a note longer than four counts? One way to do that is with a **tie.** A tie is a curved line that connects two notes that are the same pitch.

When you encounter a tie, you hold the note for the total sum of the two values but *do not play it twice.* In the example above, the two notes are a whole note (4) and a half note (2), so you hold the B for six counts.

A **slur** looks very similar to a tie, but there is one big difference: a slur connects two notes that are *different* pitches.

A slur indicates that you should play the two notes smoothly, or **legato.** This is another term you can add to the list of articulations you learned in Unit 2.

Ties and slurs affect accidentals in different ways as well. Remember that a measure line usually cancels all accidentals that are found in the previous measure. If a note is tied across a measure line, however, the accidental remains in effect.

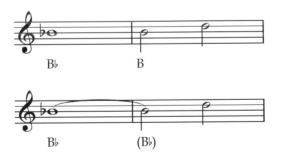

Without the tie, the B flat returns to B after the bar line. When the notes are tied, however, it remains B flat.

Repeats

A musician's time is as valuable as anyone else's, so if a composer would like a performer to play something again, they might use a **repeat sign** instead of writing out the entire thing twice. Repeat signs look like a final double bar with two dots.

If you see the repeat sign, you always go back to beginning unless there is a **beginning repeat sign**. This looks the same as the symbol above, only facing the opposite way.

In the case of music that has both symbols, you only repeat the music that is between the two repeat signs.

Imagine you want most of the music played the same, but you would like the ending to be different. In that case, you can use 1st and 2nd endings.

In the example above, you would play the first four measures, then repeat back to the beginning like usual. However, the second time you play the passage you would skip the fourth measure and only play measure five.

The numbers you see above the music are called **measure numbers**. I've included them here so it's easier to explain the order you would play this music. The order, in measure numbers, would be:

$$1 - 2 - 3 - 4 - 1 - 2 - 3 - 5$$

Repeats can be a very useful tool when writing music, and they save paper, too! As you practice the exercises in the workbook, remember what you have learned in this chapter and it will not be long before you feel comfortable with everything.

3.3 Keyboard Skills

Now that you've learned the basic fingerings for the right hand and left hand, let's do some practice with sharps and flats. To warm up, though, try practicing some of the white-key patterns that you learned in the last unit. Be sure to use correct fingerings!

After practicing this a few times, try the same pattern but starting on the note G. All the fingerings will remain the same, you are simply starting on a different note.

Feel comfortable? Let's introduce the black keys into the mix.

Patterns with Sharps

For these exercises, we'll use the same five-finger/five-note pattern that you have been playing. Watch out for the black keys, though – you may have to adjust your hand position slightly. Try the right hand first. For this pattern, your thumb will need to start on the note D.

Now try the left hand. This time, your pinky will start on D.

When you're comfortable, play both hands together.

Patterns with Flats

Let's take a look at some patterns that involve flats. Starting with the right hand, your thumb will be placed on F.

With your left hand, your pinky will be on F.

When you're comfortable, try both hands together.

Let's explore on more pattern with flats. Below is the two-handed pattern, but feel free to practice one hand at a time until you are comfortable. Take special note of where the pattern begins – you'll be starting on a black key this time.

Great work! Practice these exercises until you feel comfortable. In addition, there are more exercises in the workbook to help you master these skills.

3.4 Aural Skills

We'll continue our ear training by practicing rhythms in different time signatures. The exercises will be in 2/4, 3/4, and 4/4, and they will also include rests. As with the last chapter, some of the workbook questions will ask you to recognize what rhythm is being played. In others, you will hear a rhythm and be asked to write it down or complete the measure. Continue to count out loud and pay special attention to the times that there is no sound, indicating a rest.

3.5 Music Appreciation

We said that accidentals are pitches between the natural notes. How is it possible that there are notes between the notes?

One way to answer that is by looking at how music is made in the first place. Sound is created by vibration, and different instruments have various vibrating parts that make this possible. On instruments such as the violin or guitar, a string is vibrating to make sound.

Imagine you are holding a rubber band very tightly. If you pluck it, you will create a high, twangy sound. Now loosen your grip a little and pluck it again. You'll notice the sound is lower than the original pitch. Finally, hold the rubber band at a medium tension and the sound will be somewhere in between the first two.

This is essentially the same way a string instrument makes sound. If you play a guitar string with your finger high on the neck, it will produce a high sound. If you put your finger lower on the fretboard, the sound will also be lower. The reason this happens is because you are changing the length of the string. The shorter a string, the higher the sound.

Try playing the keys of a piano one by one, starting from the lowest note on the right side and going all the way to the highest note on the right side. If you open the lid of a grand piano, you can see the reason the notes sound higher is because the strings are getting shorter.

Most music we listen to only consists of natural notes and their sharp or flats. These are called **half steps**, and we will learn more about them in the next unit. However, music from many ethnic cultures uses pitches that are *even smaller* and can be found between the half steps. These are known as quarter tones or microtones and can create some very interesting sounds.

3.6 Research and Discussion

We've already learned several rhythmic concepts, so by now you know how important rhythm is to music. Without rhythm, the notes and pitches would just be a jumble of unintelligible sounds, like the static of a radio when it's not tuned to a station. Find a piece of music that has a good rhythmic element and think about the following:

- Describe the rhythmic elements.

- How is the rhythm created in this music?

- What instruments are used to create the rhythmic elements?

- Can you interpret the rhythmic pattern using note values?

- How does the vocal line compliment or compare with the rhythmic elements?

- Why do you like (or not like) this music?

3.7 Vocabulary

The following words pertaining to music were used in this unit. Look back through the chapter to find definitions and to make sure you understand them. An excellent online dictionary can be found at: http://www.music.vt.edu/musicdictionary

Accidental

Sharp

Flat

Natural

Enharmonic

Rest

Tie

Slur

Repeat Sign

1st and 2nd Endings

Measure Numbers

Unit 4

"If music be the food of love,
play on."

~ William Shakespeare, Twelfth Night

Unit 4

Distances between notes are called **intervals**. This is a large topic that we'll be coming back to later in the book, but for now we're going to learn the basics of how to calculate musical distances: half steps and whole steps. These will be the building blocks of many things to come: major scales, minor scales, chords, and much more.

4.1 Theory

Half Steps

Using the piano keyboard as a visual reference, the distance between two keys is called a **half step**. Half steps can occur two white keys or a white key and a black key.

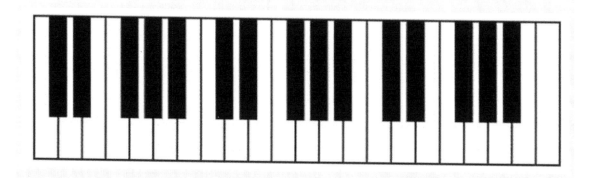

Now that you're familiar with the entire keyboard, including accidentals, you can see that there are an abundance of half steps throughout the piano. Take note of two in particular – B to C and E to F. These are the only white keys on the piano that do not have a black key between them.

Chromatic Scale

A **scale** is a pattern of notes presented in a specific order. There are many kinds of scales, and we will be talking about several throughout this book. The first one we will learn is called the **chromatic scale**. The chromatic scale is a scale made entirely of half steps from beginning to end. When playing this scale on the keyboard, you will be using every key, both black and white. In music, chromatic scales are not used as frequently as some of the other scales we will learn, however, being familiar with them will facilitate other aspects of music.

Before we learn exactly what a chromatic scale is, let's talk about some rules that apply to all scales:

- Scales can ascend or descend. When a scale ascends, it goes from a lower note to a higher note. When it descends, it goes from a higher note to a lower note.

- Scales begin and end on the same letter name. This doesn't mean it has to be the exact pitch – remember how many Cs there are on the piano? – but if a scale begins on C, it should also end on C.

A chromatic scale has 12 *different* notes. Let's try building one by starting on C. A half step up from C is C sharp, another half step is D. If you continue up in this manner, your scale should look like this:

As you can see, there are quite a bit of sharps – but take notice of where the sharps are absent. Remember that there are no black keys between E and F or B and C. This is very important when writing chromatic scales. If you write E sharp followed by F, what will it sound like?

One thing that makes the chromatic scale unique is that you use sharps when writing ascending scales, but you use flats when writing descending scales. To create a descending scale, again start on C. A half step below C is B, followed by B flat. Your complete scale should look like this:

Again, notice where there are *no* flats. If you write C flat followed by B, what will it sound like?

Your complete C chromatic scale, ascending with sharps and descending with flats, will look like this:

A chromatic scale can begin on any note, but when building them remember to follow the guidelines above. Here are a couple of more chromatic scales for you to compare.

- F Chromatic Scale:

- A Chromatic Scale

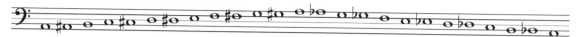

Play through some of these so you can hear them. Although they might sound unusual, they can be a lot of fun to play and give music an interesting twist.

Whole Steps

A **whole step** is the distance of two keys on the piano. Whole steps can occur between two white keys, two black keys, or a black key and a white key.

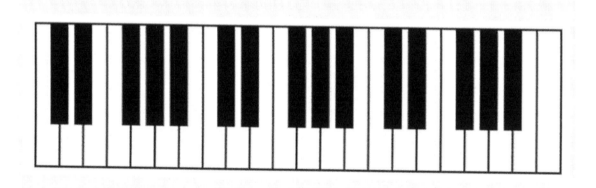

Looking at the keyboard, you can see that from C to D is a whole step, and C sharp to D sharp is also a whole step. However, again take notice of those specials pairs of notes (E/F and B/C). Starting on E, for example, a whole step up would be F sharp.

Whole-Tone Scale

A **whole-tone scale** is a scale made entirely of whole steps. Like chromatic scales, these are not used as frequently as some other scales, but are nonetheless good educational tools. They are also a little more complicated to build than chromatic scales, but not so difficult if you follow the guidelines.

A whole-tone scale only has six different notes. Starting on the note C, a whole step up will be D, followed by E. Here is where you have to be careful, though – the next whole step is F sharp.

Your complete C whole-tone scale will look like this:

Notice what looks like a gap between the A sharp and C. Although this looks strange, if you look at a keyboard, you can easily see that the distance between the two notes is a whole step. This is what makes writing whole-tone scales difficult – you must always remember what is a whole step and what is not.

When writing these scales, be aware that it's best to use either only flats or only sharps. Try not to mix them within the same scale, as you did with chromatic scales. This will give you the best practice identifying whole steps.

Try building some other whole-tone scales. For comparison, here are two more for you to look at (remember to pay attention to the "gaps"):

- G Whole-Tone Scale

- E♭ Whole-Tone Scale

As with chromatic scales, these may sound a bit unusual to your ears, but they create some great sounds and can be fun to play.

4.2 Rhythm

Along with rhythmic values that equal 1, 2, 3, and 4 counts, there is also a note value that is equal to ½ of a beat. These are called **eighth notes.**

Eighth Notes

An eighth note is equal to ½ of a count. They fit into the "rhythm tree" like this:

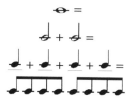

Displayed in this manner, you can see why they are called eighth notes – Eight of them are equal to a single whole note.

Eighth notes can look a couple of different ways. If there is a single eighth note, it looks like a quarter note with a flag.

If there are two or more eighth notes in a row, they will often be connected with a **beam.**

Usually more than four will be separated by a space, like you see in the diagram above. To help count eight notes, you can say "1 & 2 & 3 & 4 &." Many people also use their foot to help. When your toe touches the ground, that would be a numbered count, when the toe is in the air, it would be an "&."

1 & 2 & 3 & 4 &

If you incorporated other rhythms into the passage, you might count it something like this:

1 & 2 & 3 & 4 &   1 & 2 & 3 & 4 &   1 & 2 &3 &4   &   1&2&3&4&

50

The secret to counting passages with eighth notes – or any musical passage, for that matter – is to always keep a steady beat. Notice in the example above that, even though there are a variety of note values, you constantly count the eighth notes.

Eighth Rests

If eighth notes exist, then you can also have **eighth rests**. An eighth rest look like this: ⅞

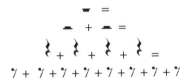

Unlike eighth notes, there is only one way to write an eighth rest, because if you need to rest longer than a single eighth note, you would simply use a larger rest value.

In music, you should count eighth rests the same way you count eighth notes (1 & 2 &, etc.). Remember to always keep a steady pulse.

As you practice the exercises found in the workbook, be sure to keep a steady pulse.

51

4.3 Keyboard Skills

In the last unit we started to use the black keys of the piano. These are a little more complicated than just playing white keys, but they are of course necessary to make music interesting and give a lot of possibilities for variety. Chromatic scales are a great way to practice using accidentals, because they incorporate a lot of sharps and flats.

RH Chromatic Scale Patterns

As always, you'll want to practice these one at a time first. Since these are a little more complicated that what you have done before, let's break the scales up into segments. Pay close attention to the fingerings – they will make it much easier for you.

Right Hand:

Segment 1:

Segment 2:

Segment 3:

Segment 4:

Entire Scale:

Left Hand:

Segment 1:

Segment 2:

Segment 3:

Segment 4:

Entire Scale:

Both Hands:

I know this is difficult stuff, and don't worry if you can't get it with 100% accuracy. The exercises found in the workbook will mostly be using the short segments above. As always, just have fun with the material and do your best.

4.4 Aural Skills

We've been focusing on rhythm for the last few chapters – now we'll go back to listening to pitches. Since you've learned the difference between a half step and a whole step, try identifying them by ear. Here are a couple of tips to helps you out:

- A half step sounds like the famous *Jaws* movie theme:

- A whole step sounds like the first two notes of *Frère Jacques:*

The more you practice hearing these, the easier they will become to identify. Take a look at the exercises in the workbook to help strengthen your ear.

4.5 Music Appreciation

Instruments, especially orchestral instruments, are typically divided into four families: strings, woodwinds, brass, and percussion. We learned previously that sound is made by vibration, and each of these groups has a unique way to produce that vibration.

Strings

Strings are instruments such as violin, viola, cello, and guitar. As the name implies, they are instruments that utilize strings. Although the sound always comes from the string itself, there are many different ways to play the instruments. Violins, violas, and celli are typically played with a **bow**. Guitars, mandolins, and banjos, on the other hand, are played by plucking the strings with fingers or a **pick**. If you've ever opened up the lid of a grand piano, you know that pianos also have strings, and in this case the sound is made by a small hammer hitting the string when you play a key.

Many pieces of music have been written for a grouping called a **string quartet**, which includes two violins, viola, and cello. Strings are an important part of the orchestra, and can be used to play melodic lines, create textures, and lush harmonies. String instruments such as the violin (a.k.a. the fiddle) are also used in popular music, in particular folk styles such as country and bluegrass. The guitar is an instrument that crosses many boundaries, and is used prolifically in rock, folk, and classical styles around the world.

Woodwinds

Woodwinds are instruments that are blown to produce sound, such as the flute, saxophone, clarinet, and oboe. In the past, these instruments were made of wood, but some modern versions, such as the flute, are made of metal. The sound of flute is created by blowing across the edge of a hole, but instruments such as the saxophone and oboe utilize **reeds**. A reed is a small piece of material that vibrates when blown to produce sound.

Woodwinds can be found in a variety of musical genres. In addition to orchestras, there are wind ensembles and wind quintets that frequently perform, and woodwinds are an important part of musical traditions around the world. The flute, for example, is used in the music of Ireland, Africa, the Appalachians, and Native Americans, to name a few. Clarinets have also been used in Big Band music as well as the Jewish Klezmer styles.

Brass

Instruments in the **brass** family include the trumpet, trombone, and tuba. Typically, as the name implies, these instruments are made of brass. Like woodwinds, sound is also produced by blowing into these instruments, except the player must also make a vibrating sound with their lips (similar to what is often referred to as a "raspberry" in the non-musical world).

Brass instruments are found in a lot of "heroic" orchestral music, such as the music of Beethoven and the Americana sounds of Aaron Copland. If you watch movies about national heroes, sport heroes, or individuals that triumphantly overcome challenges, you will surely hear a lot of brass. However, brass instruments are also a staple of jazz and Big Band music. Musicians such as Miles Davis and Dizzy Gillespie, for instance, championed the trumpet and inspired many young musicians to play.

Percussion

Perhaps the largest of all categories, **percussion** instruments include drum sets, bongos, congos, handbells, shakers, vibrophones, and much, much more. Almost anything can be made into a percussion instrument – performers throughout the years have used anything from washboards to trashcans to make a beat. Many percussion instruments are hit with a stick or mallet, but they can also make sound by being shaken or rubbed.

Percussion instruments are the foundation of almost all music genres, whether it's rock, folk, classical, jazz, or world music. Without a good rhythm section, a lot of music just doesn't make sense.

Keyboards

We've already mentioned the piano in the string family, but **keyboard** instruments can also be considered to be in their own category. The reason is that most keyboard instruments are more complex in the way they make sound and they don't all follow the same rules. A piano, for instance, has strings, but the sound is made by hitting it them like a percussion instrument. On the other hand, an organ makes sound by pushing air through large pipes, similar to woodwind instruments.

Other keyboard instruments include the harpsichord, clavichord, and even the accordion. Because of the variety of instruments within this category, keyboards are an important ingredient in almost every musical genre.

Electronic Instruments

Changes in technology and the way music is made now demands an additional category: Electronic instruments. Sounds from these instruments are created by sending electronic signals through speakers. One of the earliest electronic instruments was an invention called the **Theremin**, which was played by the performer moving their hands between what looks like radio antennas and created an eerie, mysterious sound.

Electronic instruments have since come a long way, and synthesizers, computers, and other digital products are commonplace on the music scene today. Some electronic instruments are digital replications of traditional instruments, and others are completely unique unto themselves.

4.6 Research and Discussion

After reading about the instrument families in the Music Appreciation section, select an instrument you like and think about the following ideas:

- What instrument family does it belong to?

- What do you like about this instrument?

- What kind of music utilizes this instrument?

- Who are some important performers that played this instrument?

- What composers have written for this instrument?

- Find a piece of music that showcases this instrument.

- Why do you think this piece of music was written for this particular instrument?

- Do you think this music is appropriate for this instrument?

- Can you find examples of this instrument being used in an unusual way?

4.7 Vocabulary

The following words pertaining to music were used in this unit. Look back through the chapter to find definitions and to make sure you understand them. An excellent online dictionary can be found at: http://www.music.vt.edu/musicdictionary

Half step

Chromatic scale

Whole step

Whole-tone scale

Eighth note

Beam

Eighth rest

Strings

Woodwinds

Brass

Percussion

Keyboard

Electronic instruments

Unit 5

"Without music, life would be an error.
The German imagines even God singing songs."

~ Friedrich Nietzsche

Unit 5

Up to now you have learned what might be referred to as the "fundamentals" of music. That is, basic elements of music that don't mean much on their own, but once combined create something worth listening to. If you think of our analogy of a building, you have now learned about screws, nails, wood, metals, etc. Now we're going to start building the actual foundation and framework.

5.1 Theory

Major Scales

As you already learned, there are many different kinds of scales. The very foundation of most music as we know it is based the **major scale**. Why is it so important? Many people loathe major scales because they are made to practice them over and over when they learn instruments, but the truth of the matter is that major scales provide the reference point for almost every aspect of music, from the melodies that are sung to the harmonies that are played and nearly everything else in between. To being with, we'll just be learning what a major scale is, but as you continue your studies you will see how they continue to appear again and again.

Major scales are a specific pattern of whole steps *and* half steps. This is different from the other two scales you have learned (The chromatic scale is purely half steps and the whole-tone scale is only whole steps). But although this might make it sound more complicated, once you have learned the pattern it will be easy to apply and build any major scale you desire.

The best way to find the pattern is by starting with the C major scale. Let's look at the piano and find the note C.

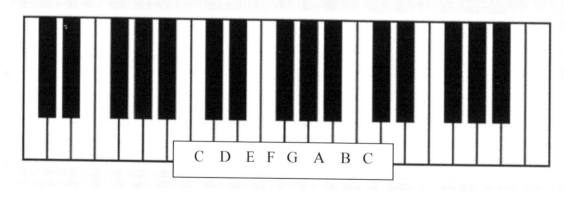

If you play white keys starting on C going all the way up to the next highest C, you will hear a very familiar sound, as you have no doubt heard the major scale many times before. Since we don't have to deal with sharps or flats, this makes it a good place to start.

60

To find the pattern, simply identify the distance between each note. C-D, for example, is a whole step (W), D-E is also a whole step, and E-F is a half step (H). If you continue, the pattern should be:

W – W – H – W – W – W – H

Memorize this pattern – it is (and will continue to be) essential to building major scales.

Before we move on, let's talk about some additional guidelines for creating major scales. You will recognize some of these from the last unit.

Major Scales:

- Always have a pattern of W-W-H-W-W-W-H
- Always begin and end on the same note
- Never combine sharps and flats in the same scale (specifically for major scales)
- Must use each note letter name once in alphabetical order
- May not repeat a letter name unless all seven have been used

---

Shortly we'll be incorporating accidentals – this makes building scales more complicated, but it will be easier if you remember the above guidelines.

Major Scales with Sharps

Let's try building another major scale, this time starting on G. If you follow the white keys, you'll soon see that something interesting happens towards the end of the scale.

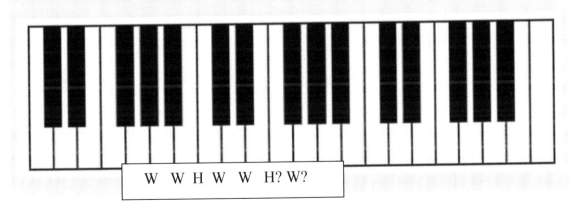

W W H W W H? W?

Try playing these notes and you'll notice that they sound different – not necessarily bad, but it doesn't resemble the major scale sound that you are familiar with. Why is this?

Remember the pattern (W-W-H-W-W-W-H) of a major scale. This works for most of scale, but you can see above that E-F is a half step, which does not follow the pattern. To correct this, raise F to F♯. We now have the whole step that we need, and everything works out perfectly because we also have the next half step required, from F♯-G. The G major scale, therefore, looks like this:

Try building a major scale starting on D. As you go through the notes, you'll find a couple of places you'll need to make adjustments. The final D major scale will look like this:

Now that you know the pattern for a major scale and you see how accidentals are used, try building scales starting on A, E, and B for extra practice.

Major Scales with Flats

Not all major scales use sharps – some require flats to function correctly. Let's try building a scale starting on F. As with the scales you just made, you'll notice some places that will need to be adjusted.

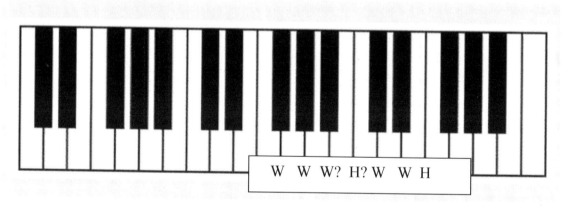

This time, A-B is a whole step, and we actually need a half step. To make this happen, lower B down to B♭. This gives us the half step we need, as well as the whole step required from B♭-C. The rest of the scale works out fine, and your complete F major scale looks like this:

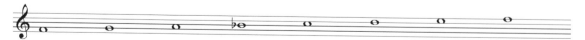

The scales in the preceding section used sharps, so why don't we use sharps here? If we called the note A♯, it would still create the ½ step we need, but we would have used the letter "A" twice. In addition, the next written note would be C, meaning we would have skipped the letter "B" entirely. Although the scale would *sound* the same, if you remember the guidelines for major scales, you'll note that neither of these is acceptable. This can be a difficult idea to grasp, but think of it like using correct grammar. Although writing it a certain way doesn't necessarily change the sound, it does provide a standard that can be read by musicians worldwide.

Try creating a major scale starting on B♭. For this one in particular, remember that the note you end on must be the same as your first note (B♭ – not B).

Now that you have the hang of this, try building E♭, A♭, and D♭ major scales.

Scale Degrees

The notes of a scale can be referred to as **degrees**. The first degree of a scale is the first note, the second degree is the second note, etc. Instead of using this ordinal language, however, the degrees of a scale can be called by specific names.

> 1st **Degree – Tonic**
> 2nd **Degree – Supertonic**
> 3rd **Degree – Mediant**
> 4th **Degree – Subdominant**
> 5th **Degree – Dominant**
> 6th **Degree – Submediant**
> 7th **Degree – Leading Tone**

The catch, however, is that you must always match the names to the scale that you are using. For example, the tonic of a C major scale is "C" because it is the first note of the scale, and the tonic of a G major scale is "G." Following this logic, the mediant of a C major scale is "E" and the mediant of a G major scale is "B."

5.2 Rhythm

Remember the dotted half note that you learned? In this unit we'll be using the dot yet again.

The Dotted Quarter Note

The dotted half note was three counts, but remember that the dot doesn't mean three – it instructs you to increase the value of the note by ½. The dot, therefore, can actually be applied to any note value.

A common use of the dot is with the quarter note. Let's figure this out using musical math.

$$= \quad + \quad = \quad 1\,\tfrac{1}{2}$$

(original note value)   (½ of original value)

This is the formula for a **dotted quarter note**. In music, it is often coupled with an eighth note in the following way:

1 & 2 & 1 & 2 &

Practice some rhythms in the workbook using dotted quarter notes.

5.3 Keyboard Skills

The 5-note exercises you played in Units 2 and 3 are actually the first half of major scales. In this unit we'll learn fingerings for the full scales.

RH Major Scale Patterns

Just like we broke the chromatic scales into segments, we'll do the same thing for major scales. Again, pay close attention to the fingerings because they will facilitate the movements.

Right Hand:

Segment 1:

Segment 2:

Entire Scale:

Left Hand:

Segment 1:

Segment 2:

Entire Scale:

Both Hands:

Once you feel comfortable with this material, take a look at the exercises in the workbook. They will give you practice playing patterns with the C major scale. As before, most of the work will be involving the short segments above, so don't worry if you aren't playing the whole scale perfectly.

5.4 Aural Skills

Thus far, we have been discussing ways to train your ear to recognize what it hears. Now let's take a different approach – we want to learn how to look at a piece of music and know what it will sound like. To do this, we're going to talk about **sight singing** and **solfège**. If singing out loud scares you, don't get too frightened – the goal of this isn't necessarily to make you a singer, it's to teach you how to look at music and hear it in your head.

Solfège refers to syllables that are sometimes used to refer to notes. You have probably heard the song that goes "Doe: a deer, a female deer; Ray: a drop of golden sun," etc. The syllables in that song are solfège.

The general idea of solfège is that these syllables are assigned to notes of a scale. Below is a list of solfège syllables.

Do (pronounced "doe") = First note of scale
Re (pronounced "ray") = Second note of scale
Mi (pronounced "me") = Third note of scale
Fa (pronounced "fa") = Fourth note of scale
Sol (pronounced "so") = Fifth note of scale
La (pronounced "la") = Sixth note of scale
Ti (pronounced "tee") = Seventh note of scale
Which, as the song goes, brings us back to "**Do**" - we are again at the beginning of the scale

In the C major scale, the solfège syllables would be assigned like this:

In the exercises in the workbook, you will have chance to practice working with solfège syllables. Before you try singing, practice reading the syllables by themselves. For many of you, this will be something unfamiliar – but don't be embarrassed! You'll get the hang of with a little bit of practice.

5.5 Music Appreciation

Musicians have been playing major scales for a few thousand years, but they started to establish themselves as the foundation of Western music during the Baroque era (generally considered to be 1600-1750). The most famous composer from the Baroque era is **Johann Sebastian Bach** (1685-1750). During his lifetime, J. S. Bach wrote approximately 1,200 pieces of music, most of it for churches where he was employed. He also taught lessons, was an astounding performer on organ, and was generally obsessed with music – he once walked two hundred miles to hear his favorite organist, Dietrich Buxtehude, perform.

Bach produced twenty children and was married twice, but he also had a temper. He found himself in jail more than once, and his letters show that he had many arguments with both people who owed him money and people he owed money to. He was once ambushed on the street by his students, who wanted him to apologize for insulting a fellow bassoonist. Not only did Bach not apologize; he also drew a knife to defend himself.

His music, however, is known for its musical and intellectual complexity, and one writer has called it the music of the heavens. He wrote masses, hymns, preludes, fugues, and dances, as well as an entire cantata about coffee. He wrote music for children, students, royalty, millionaire amateurs, and he continues to be one of the most popular composers performed in concert halls today. His music is also now quite literally in the heavens – three pieces by Bach were launched into space on the *Voyager* spacecraft in 1977.

5.6 Research and Discussion

Different types of scales can be associated with different feelings and emotions. The major scales are usually associated with a generally "happy" feeling. If you've heard a song that made you feel good, uplifted, or was just plain goofy, it probably used notes from a major scale.

Find a piece of music that you think uses a major scale and think about the following ideas:

- Why do you think it is using notes from a major scale?

- What kind of emotion does the music have?

- What images come to mind as you listen to this music?

- If there are words, do the words reflect what the music is expressing?

- Is the title appropriate for the music?

- What do you like (or not like) about this music?

- Do you agree that major scales generally sound happy? Why or why not?

5.7 Vocabulary

The following words pertaining to music were used in this unit. Look back through the chapter to find definitions and to make sure you understand them. An excellent online dictionary can be found at: http://www.music.vt.edu/musicdictionary

Major scale

Scale degree

Dotted quarter note

Sight singing

Solfège

Johann Sebastian Bach

Unit 6

"All music is folk music.
I ain't never heard no horse sing a song."

~ Louis Armstrong

Unit 6

When you hear someone say they are "playing in a **key**," what does that mean? It has to do with the major scales you just learned. When a piece is "in a key" it means that that *most* of the notes that are played are derived from the scale of the same name. For example, if a song is in the key of C major, most of the notes that are played can be found in the C major scale (no sharps or flats). If you play an accidental, it may not sound bad, but just might sound like an "accident."

If a piece is in the key of G major, however, it means that most of the notes come from the G major scale. How is this different from the example above? In the scale of G major, there is no F♮ – instead, you play an F♯. This may not seem like a big difference, but if you play F♮ you'll notice that it sounds a bit out of place. If you take this idea and compare various scales, you'll see that they are all different – some in small ways, others big – but not a single one is exactly the same.

6.1 Theory

Key Signatures

To help us identify keys, composers use **key signatures**. These are found on the left side of a staff after the clef sign. If there is time signature, it appears between it and the clef sign.

The basic rule for a key signature is that if there is an accidental over a line or space, that particular note is sharped or flatted throughout the *entire* piece. In the above example, there is a sharp over the line "F," so whenever you see the note F in the piece, you actually play F♯. The is true for *all* Fs, no matter where they are on the staff.

In the example above, all the notes look like F, but because of the key signature are played as F♯. What if you want to play a regular ol' F? In that case, you can use the natural sign.

Now, the first measure would be F♯, the second F♮, but the third and fourth would again be F♯ (remember that the measure line cancels the accidental from the previous measure).

These same principles to *all* sharps or flats you see in a key signature, whether they appear on the treble staff or bass staff.

Key Signatures with Sharps

There is much more to a key signature, however. In the introduction, we talked briefly about what it means to play "in a key." Let's explore that a little more.

The key signature in the example above tells us that all Fs throughout the entire piece must be sharped. What major scale has all natural notes except for F♯?

The answer is the G major scale. Using a key signature, you could write the same scale like this (the key signature tells us F is sharp, so you do not need to write another sharp sign before F):

Since you are playing notes that are derived from the G major scale, you are in the key of G major. Therefore, a single sharp in the key signature (F♯) tells you that you are key of G major.

What would the key signature look like for the key of D major?

D Major Scale:

D Major Scale with Key Signature:

All of the examples above are in the treble staff, but the same principles apply to the bass staff. Here are the same scales and key signatures in the bass clef:

G Major

D Major:

Notice in the D Major key signature that F♯ is written first, then C♯. Sharp and flats are written in a specific order or in key signatures. We'll talk about this more shortly, but for now remember that the order of the first two sharps is always F♯ then C♯.

Key Signatures with Flats

Since there are scales with flats, there are also key signatures with flats. Let's review the F major scale:

Based on what you know of key signatures, you can guess what the key signature will look like for F major:

(Treble Clef)

(Bass Clef)

Using this key signature, whenever you see a "B" you will play B♭. What is the key signature for B♭ major?

B♭ major scale:

B♭ major key signature:

(Treble Clef)

(Bass Clef)

As with sharps, flats in a key signature must be written in a specific order. B♭ is always first, and E♭ is always second.

Order of Accidentals in a Key Signature

We've only discussed a few major scales, but there are several more possibilities – all together, there are seven with sharps, and another seven for flats. Although we won't be discussing all of these in depth, let's go ahead and talk about what their key signatures will look like.

As mentioned earlier, the sharps and flats in a key signature must be written in a specific order. The order of sharps, from left to right, is:

F♯ – C♯ – G♯ – D♯ – A♯ – E♯ – B♯

You can remember this by saying:

Fat
Cats
Go
Down
Alleys
Eating
Bread

In addition to a specific order, they must also be written on specific lines and spaces:

The order for flats is:

$$B\flat - E\flat - A\flat - D\flat - G\flat - C\flat - F\flat$$

The way to remember this is:

Before
Eating
A
Doughnut
Get
Coffee
First

Flats must be written on these lines and spaces:

Writing the key signatures can be confusing at first, but the best way to learn them is to copy them over and over. I can't give you a good reason why they are written on these particular lines and spaces, but it is a standard practice that is readable by musicians worldwide.

Identifying Key Signatures with Sharps

There are good reasons that accidentals are written in this specific order, and one of them is that it makes it much easier to identify what key you are in. It's possible, of course, to go through every scale and determine what the key signature would be – but that would a somewhat time-consuming effort. To make it easier, there are tricks to help you.

To identify a key signature with sharps, look at the *last* sharp written and go up a half step.

In this key signature, the last sharp written in F♯. Go up half step, and you arrive at G. Therefore, this is the key of G major.

What key signature is this?

The last sharp written is D♯. Go up a half step, and you will find that you are in the key of E major.

There are two sharp keys you must be particularly careful with. Look at this key signature:

The last sharp written is E♯, so your first inclination might be to say that this is the key of F major. However, take a quick look at the keyboard and you'll see the problem.

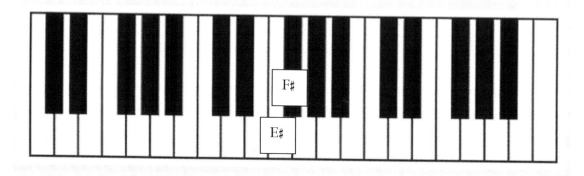

Because there is no black key between E and F, a half step up from E♯ is actually F♯. The key signature above represents the key of F♯ major. Look carefully at the key of C♯ major for the same reason:

Since the last sharp written is B♯, a half step higher would be C♯ - *not* C.

The process of identifying key signatures with flats is slightly different, but actually slightly easier. For these, look at the second-to-last flat – and that is your key. Nothing more to do.

Looking above, the second-to-last flat is B♭, so you are in the key of B♭ major. What key is this?

The second-to-last flat is D♭, so you are in the key of D♭ major.

The only flat key you must memorize is F major. Since there is only one flat in this key signature, there is no "second-to-last" flat.

There is one more key signature that we haven't discussed: C major. This one is completely different from all the others…

But I don't think it will be a problem… do you?

6.2 Rhythm

Pick-Up Notes

Take a look at this music and see if you can identify what is wrong:

Based on what we learned about time signatures, 4/4 tells us that there must be four quarter notes in each measure. The first and last measures, however, do not agree with this rule.

Incomplete measures at the beginning of music are called **pick-up notes**. In the above example, it is a quarter note, but it can be any note value or combination of note values that doesn't add up to the correct number of beats. Most of the time, the missing beats will appear in the last measure.

Pick-up notes are counted by counting *backwards* from the measure. It can also help you to look at the last measure and see what is missing. Here are a few more examples.

Pick-up notes are also called **upbeats** or **anacrusis**. Practice rhythms with these in your workbook.

6.3 Keyboard Skills

Now that you have some practice with the C major scale, let's work on a couple of scales that incorporate accidentals. The fingerings are very similar, but we will continue to break them down into segments. Remember to practice the right hand and left hand separately at first.

G Major Scale

Right Hand:

Segment 1:

Segment 2:

Entire RH Scale:
(Note key signature)

Left Hand:

Segment 1:

Segment 2:

Entire LH Scale:
(Note key signature)

Both Hands:
(Note key signature)

In your workbook, practice more exercises in the key of G major.

6.4 Aural Skills

Solfège can be used for all keys. Remember that the syllables refer to degrees of the scale, so "do" will not always be the note C. "do" is the first degree of the scale, "re" is the second degree, etc. If you apply these to different major scales, they would look like this:

G Major Scale

Do   Re   Mi   Fa   Sol   La   Ti   Do

F Major Scale

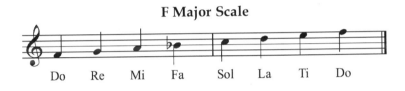

Do   Re   Mi   Fa   Sol   La   Ti   Do

D Major Scale

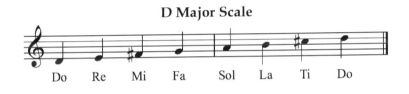

Do   Re   Mi   Fa   Sol   La   Ti   Do

B♭ Major Scale

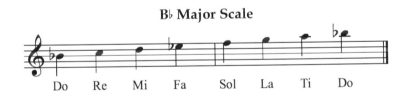

Do   Re   Mi   Fa   Sol   La   Ti   Do

This idea is called **movable do** because "do" is determined by the key. Practice solfège with various scales in your workbook. Be sure to notice what key you are in by looking at the key signature.

6.5 Music Appreciation

If learning about keys seems difficult, there may be help. In the 17th century, music theorists designed something called the **circle of 5ths** to help organize the keys. Many people still use this today, and it has become an unspoken requirement of learning music theory. The idea behind this graph is to show the relationship between keys and their key signatures. Before we discuss it, however, I want to give you a fair warning: This isn't an ultra-easy method like some of the mnemonic devices we've talked about before. It will help you, but it's going to take a little bit of effort on your part.

The circle of 5ths is based on the idea of something called an **interval**. We're going to get more in depth with intervals in the next chapter, but for now you just need to know that an interval is the distance between two notes. The circle of 5ths is created by looking at a specific interval called the 5th. Take a look at the graph below:

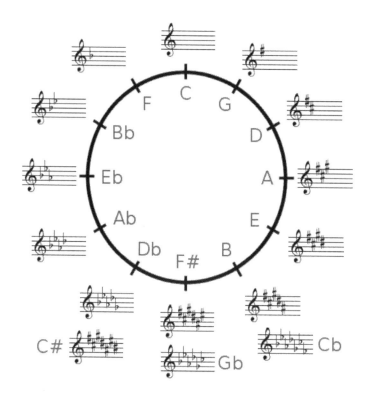

At the top, you see the key of C. To its right is the key of G. If you count from C to G, you will get a 5th:

C – D – E – F – **G**

1 – 2 – 3 – 4 – 5

If you count up five from G, you will get to D. Five more will land you on A, and so on and so forth. As we study more of the intervals, this will start to make more sense to you, but for now just focus on the fact that C has no sharps or flats in the key signature, G has one sharp, D has two sharps, etc. If you look at the left side, the same idea occurs with flats: F has one flat in the key signature, B♭ has two flats, etc.

We're not talking about this in more depth because, frankly, a lot of beginning students get confused with this material and it ends up not helping them at all. This will help you the most if you memorize it – when you're taking a test, you can write it down and refer to it for orientation. Try coming up with your own mnemonic devices to help you commit it to memory.

6.6 Research and Discussion

The interesting thing about all these keys, key signatures, and scales we've been discussing is that they are all based on the same mathematical ideas. Major scales always have a pattern of W-W-H-W-W-W-H, which means the keys and key signatures also will be based on similar patterns. In addition, major scales as a whole sound "happy," meaning that a song in C major will have very similar emotion to A major. To make it even more confusing, some major scales are enharmonic – they sound the same but can be written differently (like G♭ major and F♯ major). What, then, is the point of having all these different keys?

In many cases, certain keys are easier on some instruments rather than others. String players, for example, tend to like keys that have sharps, while woodwind and brass instruments prefer flats. This has to do with the way the instruments are built and the physical demands of the way you play them. Of course, almost everyone likes the key of C!

- Find a song you like and determine what key it is in.

- What instruments are used in this music?

- Is this an easy or difficult key to play in?

- Can you think of any reasons that it was written in this key?

- Do you hear any musical differences between various keys? If so, what differences?

6.7 Vocabulary

The following words pertaining to music were used in this unit. Look back through the chapter to find definitions and to make sure you understand them. An excellent online dictionary can be found at: http://www.music.vt.edu/musicdictionary

Key

Key signature

Pick-up note

Upbeat

Anacrusis

Movable do

Circle of 5ths

Interval

Enharmonic

Unit 7

---

*"Music washes away from the soul
the dust of everyday life."*

~ Red Auerbach

Unit 7

You recently learned that an **interval** is the distance between two notes. Like scales, there are many different kinds of intervals. Knowledge of intervals will help with song writing, ear training, and generally putting music together. We'll start off this unit by discussing two different kinds of intervals.

7.1 Theory

Intervals

Intervals are calculated numerically by ordinal numbers. The distance from C to E, for example, is a "3rd," from G to D a "5th." To find the appropriate number, simply start counting from the first note with the number 1.

C – D – E
1   2   3

G – A – B – C – D
1 2 3 4 5

This is of course a simple concept, but many people get confused when they forget to give the first note "1." Instead, they begin counting with the second note, which, in the example above, would result in a 4th. This is incorrect – G to D is a 5th.

G – A – B – C – D
1 2 3 4 - WRONG

The numerical part of an interval's name is always calculated from the lowest note. C-G is a 5th, however, G-C is a 4th.

5th   4th

Interval names are also related to their letter names. C-G is a 5th, but so is C-G♯ and C-G♭ because all three have the letter "G." C-A, C-A♭ and C-A♯ are all 6ths because all three contain the letter "A."

C♯ D♯ E♯ F♯ G♯ A♯ B♯ C♯
C♭ D♭ E♭ F♭ G♭ A♭ B♭ C♭
C – D – E – F – G – A – B – C
1 2 3 4 5 6 7 8

Note that even though A♭ and G♯ are enharmonic notes – they sound the same – they are not the same interval. This is another example of using "correct grammar."

There are two exceptions to the numerical names:

1. Two notes of the exact same pitch are not called a "1st," they are called **unison**.
2. Two notes that have the same letter, but one is higher or lower, is not called an "8th" it is called an **octave**.

F – G – A – B – C – D – E - F
1   8
Unison   Octave

Major Intervals

Although F-A, F-A♯, and F-A♭ are all 3rds, they are all different kinds of 3rds. The kind of interval is called the **quality**.

Major intervals are derived from the major scale. C-D, for example, is a **major 2nd (M2)** because D is the second note of the C major scale. C-D♯ is a 2nd, but since D♯ is not part of the scale, it is a different quality.

Looking at the C major scale, you can see that C-E is a major 3rd, C-A is a major 6th, and C-B is a major 7th. We're looking at the C major scale because C is the lowest note – but what if we start on a different note?

Let's look at the G major scale.

In this case, G-A is a major 2nd, G-B is a major 3rd, and G-E is a major 6th – but pay close attention to the major 7th. It's not G-F, It's G-F♯. Because F♯ is the 7th note of the G major scale, it is a major interval. As before, G-F is a 7th but a different quality.

When building intervals, always refer to the major scale of the lowest note. This will help you determine the quality.

Perfect Intervals

You probably noticed that a few of the intervals were left out in the discussion of major intervals. This is because only 2nds, 3rds, 6ths, and 7ths can be major. The remaining intervals (Unison, 4th, 5th, and Octave) are also derived from the major scale, but they have a different name: **perfect**.

The process for finding perfect intervals is the same as for major intervals. Look at the major scale for the lower of the two notes. C-G is a **perfect 5th** because G is the 5th note of the C major scale. C-G♯ is a 5th, but a different quality.

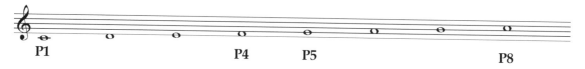

Again, when finding perfect intervals you must be cognizant of the major scale for the lower of the two notes. What is a perfect 4th up from F?

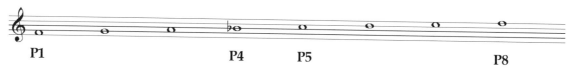

B♭ is the 4th note of the F major scale, so F- B♭ is a **perfect 4th**.

7.2 Rhythm

Just as there are different kinds of scales, key signatures, and intervals, there are also different kinds of time signatures. You have already learned 2/4, 3/4, and 4/4, but these all have the same bottom number. This unit we will begin discussing time signatures that have a different bottom number than you've seen before.

Time Signatures

You have already learned that the bottom number is a code that represents a specific note value. If 4 equals quarter note, what do you think 2 represents?

A 2 on the bottom of a time signature represents a half note. A time signature of 4/2, for example, would mean there are four half notes in a measure.

There is a catch, however: In 4/4 and the other time signatures we learned, the half note received 2 counts. When two is the bottom number, however, the half note receives *one* count.

If the half note receives 1 count, how do you count a whole note?

And what about quarter notes?

There's that musical math again.

Common Time and Cut Time

4/4 time signature is often known as **common time** because it's the most commonly used. If you start paying attention to the music you listen to, you will probably find that 95% of it is in 4/4. In the time signature, it is often abbreviated with a "C."

Because 2/2 is "half" of 4/4 (at least it looks that way), it is known as **cut time**. To represent cut time, you will often see a "C" with a line through it.

Although music in 4/4 and 2/2 look very similar, it must be counted different. Remember what note gets the count of one when the bottom number is "2."

7.3 Keyboard Skills

You've practiced playing sharps in scales, but let's take a look at a scale with flats. This scale will use a slightly different fingering, so pay attention.

F Major Scale

Right Hand:

Segment 1:

Segment 2:

Entire RH Scale:
(Note key signature)

Left Hand:

Segment 1:

Segment 2:

Entire LH Scale:
(Note key signature)

Both Hands:
(Note key signature)

In your workbook, practice more exercises in the key of F major.

7.4 Aural Skills

One of the best ways to train your ear is by listening for intervals. You've already started to do this a little bit by identifying half steps and whole steps in Unit 4. Let's now practice listening for major and perfect intervals.

A major 2nd is another way of identifying a whole step. Major 2nds sound like the beginning of *Frère Jacques:*

A major 3rd sounds like the first two notes of *When the Saints Go Marching In:*

When you hear a perfect 4th, think of the *Bridal Chorus.* It's also the beginning of *O Christmas Tree* and *Amazing Grace:*

Bridal Chorus/O Christmas Tree   *Amazing Grace*

A movie theme, *Star Wars*, will remind you of a perfect 5th:

The musical cue of NBC creates a major 6th:

One of the most difficult intervals to recognize is the major 7th. A good reference for this is the beginning vocals of Led Zeppelin's *Immigrant Song* (first and third note). You can also identify it because it really feels like it wants to resolve up to the octave.

Identifying these intervals will be difficult at first, but if you use the music references above it will help out quite a bit. Practice this and train your ear with the exercises in the workbook.

7.5 Music Appreciation

As you learned this unit, both major and perfect intervals are found and derived from the major scale. This may cause you to wonder why only certain intervals are called "perfect." To answer this question, let's take a brief detour into the science class.

Sound is caused by vibration (for example, a vibrating string on a violin or guitar). As the object vibrates, it causes the air around it to vibrate, and eventually the vibrating air reaches our ears and we hear a sound. The number of vibrations per second is called a **frequency** and is measured in **hertz** (Hz). For example, a sound with 100Hz consists of 100 vibrations per second. Pitches that vibrate more frequently and have a higher Hz number sound higher in pitch (such as a flute) and pitches that vibrate less frequently and have a lower Hz number sound lower it pitch (like a trombone).

The note A440 is often used as a reference point for tuning and other measurements. This refers to the note A, which vibrates at 440Hz. What note do you think is at 880Hz? It turns out to also be the note A, but an octave higher. Therefore, the note A an octave lower would be measured at 220Hz.

Therefore, an octave has the ratio of 1:2 (i.e., 440:880 in a simplified form). All octaves have the same ratio, no matter what the pitches are.

Perfect intervals are so named because they are pairs of notes that create the simplest ratios. A perfect fifth has a ratio of 2:3, and a perfect fourth is 3:4. In addition, when the notes are inverted, they remain perfect. For example, "F-C" is a **perfect** 5th, and "C-F" is a **perfect** 4th. Notice that when you invert a major interval, it does not remain major. "C-D" is a **major** 2nd, but "D-C" is **not** a major 7th. We'll learn what it is called in the next unit.

7.6 Research and Discussion

A lot of music written in the Middle Ages was **plainchant**, sometimes called **Gregorian Chant** because the music was compiled by Pope Gregory I. This music, and music inspired by it, often uses the perfect intervals and invokes a resonant, peaceful, open sound. Most of the music in the Middle Ages was written for the church, and if you hear a piece of plainchant you can imagine it would sound incredible performed in a large, open cathedral with sound resonating around the room.

Plainchant music is still performed today, sometimes in Catholic churches as part of Mass, other times in concert halls as part of secular programs. Chant is also incorporated in to movie scores and has even been used by DJs, who have given it a modern twist by remixing sounds that originated thousands of years ago.

- How does plainchant make you feel? What emotions does it invoke?

- Find a piece of modern music that incorporates plainchant.

- How is this music inspired by plainchant?

- Can you think of modern music that does not use plainchant, but is similar to plainchant?

- The texts of plainchant are usually in Latin. Why?

- How does plainchant compare to instrumental music written in the Middle Ages?

7.7 Vocabulary

The following words pertaining to music were used in this unit. Look back through the chapter to find definitions and to make sure you understand them. An excellent online dictionary can be found at: http://www.music.vt.edu/musicdictionary

Interval

Unison

Octave

Major interval

Perfect interval

Common time

Cut time

Frequency

Hertz

Plainchant

Gregorian Chant

Unit 8

*"It's easy to play any musical instrument:
all you have to do is touch the right key at the right time
and the instrument will play itself."*

~ J.S. Bach

Unit 8

Once you have mastered major and perfect intervals, finding the remaining qualities is much easier. This unit will discuss minor, augmented, and diminished intervals. These are a little more difficult, but can again be incorporated into many musical ideas.

8.1 Theory

Minor Intervals

When a major interval is lowered by a half step, it becomes a **minor interval**. C-E, for example, is a major 3rd. If you lower E down to E♭, it becomes a **minor 3rd** (m3).

$$C - E = M3$$
$$C - E♭ = m3$$

Minor intervals up from C

It is important to realize that just because note is flat, it is not automatically minor – As before, you must be very cautious when incorporating accidentals. A minor interval is created by *lowering a major interval by a half step*. Note the major and minor 7th in the first example below.

Minor intervals up from G

Minor intervals up from F

Minor intervals up from D

100

Minor intervals up from B♭

M2   m2   M3   m3   M6   m6   M7   m7

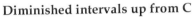

Diminished Intervals

Only major intervals become minor intervals. When lowering a perfect interval by a half step, it is called **diminished**. C-G is a perfect 5th. If G is lowered to G♭, it is a **diminished 5th** (**dim 5**).

$$C - G = P3$$
$$C - G♭ = dim\ 5$$

Diminished intervals up from C

P4   dim 4   P5   dim 5   P8   dim 8

Diminished intervals up from G

P4   dim 4   P5   dim 5   P8   dim 8

As with minor intervals, just because you see a flat sign before a note, it is not automatically diminished. A diminished interval is created by *lowering a perfect interval by a half step*. The diminished 4th in the example below includes a symbol that we haven't discussed yet.

Diminished intervals up from F

P4   dim 4   P5   dim 5   P8   dim 8

The peculiar sign above the diminished 4th is called a **double flat**. When you lower a flatted note by a half step, it becomes double flat.

Here are some other examples of diminished intervals:

Diminished intervals up from B♭

P4   dim 4   P5   dim 5   P8   dim 8

Diminished intervals up from D

| P4 | dim 4 | P5 | dim 5 | P8 | dim 8 |

Augmented Intervals

When you *raise* either a major or a perfect interval by a half step, it becomes **augmented**.

C-E is a major 3rd. If you raise E to E♯, it becomes an **augmented 3rd (aug 3)**.

$$C - E = M3$$
$$C - E\sharp = aug\ 3$$

C-G is a perfect 5th. If you raise G to G♯, it becomes an **augmented 5th (aug 5)**.

$$C - G = P5$$
$$C - G\sharp = aug\ 5$$

Augmented intervals up from C

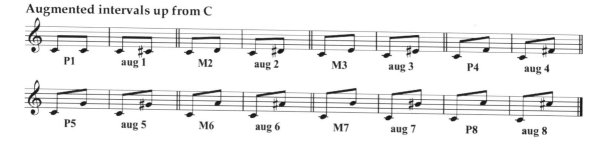

| P1 | aug 1 | M2 | aug 2 | M3 | aug 3 | P4 | aug 4 |
| P5 | aug 5 | M6 | aug 6 | M7 | aug 7 | P8 | aug 8 |

Just because a note is sharp, it doesn't necessarily mean that it is augmented. An augmented interval is created by *raising a major or perfect interval by a half step*. The augmented 7th below contains a symbol that you may not have seen before.

Augmented intervals up from G

| P1 | aug 1 | M2 | aug 2 | M3 | aug 3 | P4 | aug 4 |
| P5 | aug 5 | M6 | aug 6 | M7 | aug 7 | P8 | aug 8 |

When you raise a sharped note by a half step, it becomes **double sharp**. The symbol for a double sharp is the fancy "x" that you see above. Here are some more examples of augmented intervals:

Augmented intervals up from F

Augmented intervals up from D

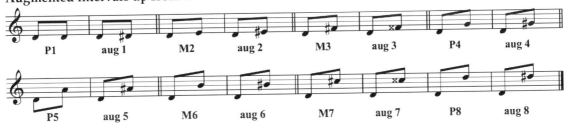

Augmented intervals up from B♭

103

Enharmonic Intervals

Just as there are enharmonic notes, there are also **enharmonic intervals**. These are intervals that *sound* the same but are *written* differently. Try playing the following intervals on the piano:

aug 4   dim 5

You will notice that you are playing the same notes, even though they have different names. Why don't they just have a single name? Yet again, it's all about using correct grammar.

Remember that one of the first ideas we talked about in this section was that the interval names are based on the letter names. C – G/G♭/G♯ are all 5ths, but different qualities of 5ths. C – F/F♭/F♯ are all 4ths, but different qualities of 4ths. By now you know the different qualities. As you learn, read, and write more music, you will see that sometimes it makes more sense to call intervals one thing over another.

What other enharmonic intervals can you find?

8.2 Rhythm

Sixteenth Notes

Eighth notes can be fast, but there are even smaller rhythmic values. Half of an eighth note is called a **sixteenth note**.

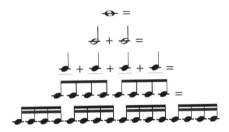

Like eight notes, you will see sixteenth notes written a variety of ways. A single sixteenth looks like an eighth with an extra flag:

Multiple sixteenths in a row are connected with two beams:

More than four are usually separated. You can count sixteenths by saying "1-e-&-a."

Sixteenth notes can be combined with other note values to create music. When counting, always keep a steady beat.

105

Sixteenth Rests

Since we have sixteenth notes, we must also have **sixteenth rests**.

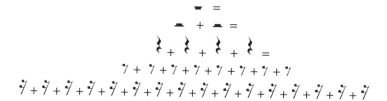

Sixteenth rests are counted the same as sixteenth notes, with a "1-e-&-a."

This new note value may appear to be fast – and in many cases, they are – but it is important to remember that the speed of music is determined by the tempo. Just like all other note values, sixteenth notes may be played at many different tempos.

8.3 Keyboard Skills

You're doing great with the scales we've learned so far, so let's up the ante a bit. The following scales will use a few extra sharps and flats.

D Major Scale

Right Hand:

Segment 1:

Segment 2:

Entire RH Scale:
(Note key signature)

Left Hand:

Segment 1:

Segment 2:

Entire LH Scale:
(Note key signature)

Both Hands:
(Note key signature)

In your workbook, practice more exercises in the key of D major.

Right Hand:

Segment 1:
(Note fingering)

Segment 2:

Entire RH Scale:
(Note key signature)

Left Hand:

Segment 1:

Segment 2:
(Note fingering)

Entire LH Scale:
(Note key signature)

Both Hands:
(Note key signature)

In your workbook, practice more exercises in the key of B♭ major.

8.4 Aural Skills

Just as there are musical references for major and perfect intervals, there are also ways to help you identify minor and diminished sounds. We usually don't worry about augmented intervals, because they are enharmonically the same as others.

A minor 2nd is another way of identifying a half step. Minor 2nds sound like the famous theme from *Jaws:*

A minor 3rd sounds like the first notes of Brahms' *Lullaby*:

A diminished 4th is enharmonically the same as a major 3rd, so you don't have to learn anything new!

When you hear a diminished 5th, you might think of the *Maria* from the musical *West Side Story*. Other references are *The Simpsons* theme music and Jimi Hendrix's *Purple Haze*.

Maria/The Simpsons   Purple Haze

Minor 6ths are a little bit more difficult, but you can use the 3rd and 4th notes of *The Entertainer* as a reference.

One of the most difficult intervals to hear is the minor 7th. One reference you can use is from an old Ford commercial – "Have you driven a Ford lately?"

Can you find other musical references to help identify these intervals? Take a look at the exercises in your workbook for more practice.

8.5 Music Appreciation

We've discussed a lot of intervals over the last two units. There is a particularly fascinating interval that we haven't talked about, however, called the **tritone**.

First, the technical definition: The word tritone is more like a nickname for a specific interval. It can be written as either a diminished 5th **OR** an augmented 5th (These are enharmonic intervals, meaning they sound the same even though they are written differently.) The name itself comes from the fact that the notes are three whole steps apart.

C – F# = tritone

C – D – E – F#
W W W

Now, the more fascinating aspect: The tritone has a very interesting history. This interval, also known as the *diabolus in musica* (the devil in music), has become legendary because it has been thought to encourage impure thoughts when played, perhaps even being the devil's calling card.

Traditionally, it is usually said that fear of this interval dates back to the Middle Ages, and was even banned by the church. Modern historians, however, suggest that the tritone wasn't referred to as the *diabolus in musica* until the 18th century. As there are no mentions of this term from the Middle Ages, it is hard to know what exactly the priests and monks thought of this interval.

Satanic or not, it is indeed an unsettling sound, and many bands in the 20th century (such as Black Sabbath) capitalized on its legend. It even shows up in the opening of Jimi Hendrix's famous song *Purple Haze*, prompting one cheeky journalist to say that, although it is unlikely that Jimi knew the name of this interval, it was appropriate because when he played he sure "raised hell."

8.6 Research and Discussion

Many people see a piece of music that has a lot of sixteenth notes and get frightened because it looks like it must be played very fast. Sometimes this is true, but a sixteenth note is more that just speed and flash - it's simply another example of what we call a **division of the beat**. A division of the beat is exactly what it sounds like: separating the beat into small segments. As a college student, you're probably eating a lot of pizza. Next time you chow down, consider this scenario:

Imagine you have a small personal pizza. It comes out of the oven as a whole, round pie. You first cut it in half, leaving two large pieces. Cut it in half again, you have four pieces. Now make two more cuts so you can feed eight people, and your final four cuts leave you with 16 equal slices of pizza. Since this is a personal size pizza, you end up with 16 very small pieces and some very unhappy friends.

You and your friends probably won't be satisfied with such small portions, so you do the same thing with an extra large. You still end up with 16 equal slices of pizza, but they are much larger than before. You will leave everyone with a full belly, much happier, and a big smile on thier face.

16th notes work the same way - They are simply a whole note that has been divided into sixteen equal portions. Therefore, they are only as fast as the tempo itself. 16th notes at a *largo* tempo will be slower that 16th notes at a *vivace* tempo. They simply divide the beat into equal portions, no matter how fast or slow the tempo.

- Find a fast piece of music.

- What instruments are playing the fast notes?

- What is the music about? Is it appropriate for fast music?

- Can you find a piece of slow music that uses 16th notes?

- What do you like or not like about this music?

8.7 Vocabulary

The following words pertaining to music were used in this unit. Look back through the chapter to find definitions and to make sure you understand them. An excellent online dictionary can be found at: http://www.music.vt.edu/musicdictionary

Minor interval

Diminished interval

Double flat

Augmented interval

Double sharp

Enharmonic interval

Sixteenth note

Sixteenth rest

Tritone

Division of the beat

Unit 9

"Music is a discipline, and a mistress of order and good manners,
she makes the people milder and gentler,
more moral and more reasonable."

~Martin Luther

Unit 9

When we learned major scales, we found that pieces in major keys are usually happy. Certainly not all music is happy, though. Part of what makes music such a big part of our lives is that it can cover the entire emotional spectrum. That music can be so encompassing is comforting; it is also empowering that it has the ability to communicate in so many ways. In this unit, we'll be discussing some new scales and keys that open up possibilities for a plethora of musical emotion.

9.1 Theory

Relative Minor Keys

You have learned that the key signatures we have discussed all represent major keys. In fact, each key signature can represent two keys: a major key and a minor key. These are called **relative keys**. We'll get to what a minor key is and the kind of scale it represents, but for now let's do some practice finding the relative minor key.

Let's start with C major. To find the **relative minor**, go up a **major 6th**.

M6

C-A is a major 6th, so the key signature below can represent either C major *or* A minor. These are relative keys.

C Major
A Minor

116

Take a look at the key signatures that you have learned and see if you can find the relative minor keys.

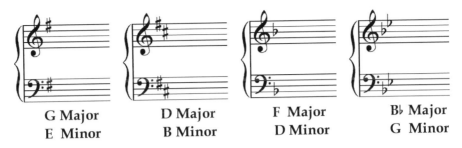

G Major
E Minor

D Major
B Minor

F Major
D Minor

B♭ Major
G Minor

Determining Keys

Your biggest question now might be how to determine whether a piece of music is in a major or minor key. One general guideline you can use is to look at the last note of the piece. That note will often be the same letter name as the key you are in.

If there are several notes played together at the end, identify the lowest of these notes and the same rule usually applies. As almost all rules have exceptions, however, so be aware that this trick is not 100% foolproof.

Both of the following examples have the same key signature. Identify the actual key by using the guideline above.

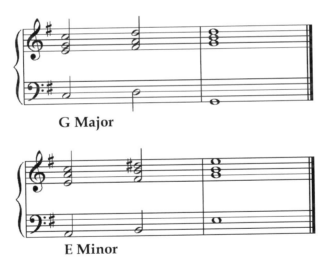

G Major

E Minor

117

Minor Scales

You can use what you know of relative keys to help you build minor scales. Simply identify the relative minor of a major key (by going up a major 6th), then write the same notes starting with that letter name. You will automatically create a minor scale.

$$C - D - E - F - G - A - B - C$$
$$(M6)$$
$$A - B - C - D - E - F - G - A$$

If you play the A minor scale written above, you will hear that it sounds quite a bit different than the C major. This is quite interesting – you are playing the exact same notes, but they have a completely different sound.

The reason it sounds different is because there is a different pattern of whole steps and half steps. The pattern for a minor scale is:

$$\mathbf{W - H - W - W - H - W - W}$$

It is possible to memorize this and create minor scales based on this pattern, however, it is more important to realize the relationship of relative keys. Practice this concept by building more minor scales. The examples below use key signatures, but you will see accidentals in parenthesis. These are called **courtesy accidentals** and are there to remind you of the sharps or flats in a key signature.

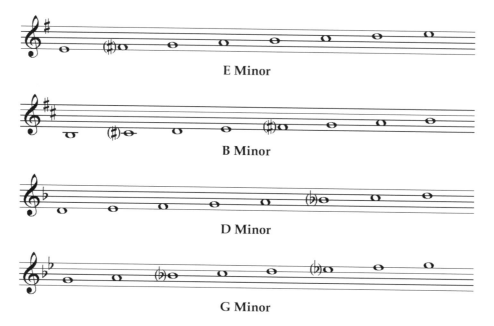

E Minor

B Minor

D Minor

G Minor

118

The scales discussed above are officially called **natural minor scales**. These scales always agree exactly with the key signature. For example, the key signature of E minor has 1 sharp (F♯), and the E minor scale also has a single sharp F♯.

As it turns out, there are two more kinds of minor scales. Both are based on the natural minor pattern, however, so make sure you are confident with building those scales first before moving on to these additional ones.

To create a **harmonic minor scale**, raise the 7th note of a natural minor scale by a half step.

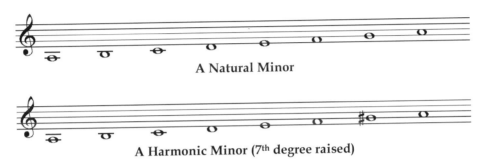

A Natural Minor

A Harmonic Minor (7th degree raised)

The harmonic minor scale has a very intriguing sound, reminiscent of gypsies or Middle Eastern music. A lot of music from Spain, especially flamenco music, contains the harmonic minor scale.

The **melodic minor scale** is the most confusing, but also the most frequently used in western classical music. To create this scale, raise the 6th *and* 7th scale degrees of the natural minor scale.

A Melodic Minor (6th and 7th degrees raised)

There is an additional catch, however. In a melodic minor scale, the 6th and 7th degrees are only raised when the scale *ascends*. The descending melodic minor scale looks exactly like the natural minor scale.

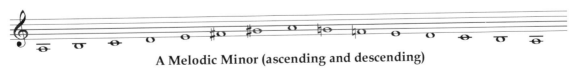

A Melodic Minor (ascending and descending)

Listen to these scales. You will hear that they all sound minor, but each has its own distinctive flavor. Although minor scales can be confusing, they add great variety and possibilities in music.

Circle of 5ths

The circle of 5ths can also be used to help you identify minor keys. As before, the best way to use this is to memorize it.

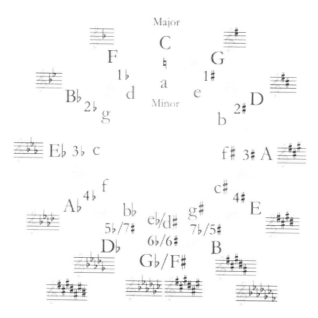

9.2 Rhythm

3/8 Time Signature

You've learned that when 4 is the bottom number of a time signature, it represents a quarter note. 2 is a half note. What would you guess an 8 represents?

The number 8 represents the eighth note. In 3/8 time, there are three eighth notes in a measure.

When we talked about cut time, you also learned that the bottom number affects the way music is counted. A time signature with 8 as the bottom number means that the eighth note receives one beat. How do you count quarter notes?

You can also use 16th notes in 3/8 time signature.

A dotted quarter note takes up 3 counts, or an entire measure.

121

6/8 Time Signature

In 6/8 time, there are 6 beats per measure and the eighth note receives one count. Music in 6/8 could look several different ways.

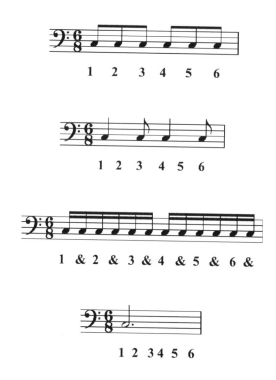

In both 3/8 and 6/8, a whole rest is used to indicate an entire measure of silence. Remember that the whole rest doesn't necessarily mean four beats.

Music in 3/8 and 6/8 time has a very dance-like feel to it. Many waltzes are in 3/8 time, and Irish music is frequently heard in 6/8 time.

9.3 Keyboard Skills

We've been spending a lot of time with major scales, so let's turn now to the darker side of music and work on the minors. Below are fingerings for the natural, harmonic, and melodic minor scales.

A Natural Minor

Right Hand:

Segment 1:

Segment 2:

Entire RH Scale:

Left Hand:

Segment 1:

Segment 2:

123

Entire LH Scale:

Both Hands:

In your workbook, practice more exercises using the A natural minor scale.

A Harmonic Minor

Right Hand:

Segment 1:

Segment 2:

Entire RH Scale:

Left Hand:

Segment 1:

Segment 2:

Entire LH Scale:

Both Hands:

In your workbook, practice more exercises using the scale of A harmonic minor.

Right Hand:

Segment 1:

Segment 2:

Entire RH Scale:

Left Hand:

Segment 1:

Segment 2:

Entire LH Scale:

Both Hands:

Remember that the melodic minor scale *descends the same as the natural minor scale*. In your workbook, practice more exercises using the scale of A melodic minor.

9.4 Aural Skills

In this section, we're going to practice identifying major and minor scales. When identifying these, think of the *character* of what you are hearing.

-   The major scale usually sounds happy

-   The natural minor scale sounds sad and melancholy

-   The harmonic minor scale sounds more aggressive, angry, and a little scary

-   The melodic minor scale starts off sad, but at the end sounds happy like a major scale

A more detailed discussion of this is in the Music Appreciation section of this unit. After reading over this material, train your ear to hear these scales by practicing with the exercises in your workbook.

9.5 Music Appreciation

When we talked about major scales, we said they could be defined as sounding happy. Although there are exceptions to every rule – sometimes music in major keys does sound sad – in general, major keys produce cheerful-sounding music. Minor scales are usually thought of as being sad, but one of the things that make the minor keys more complex is that they can cover so much emotional ground. The natural, harmonic, and melodic minor scales all sound completely different from each other, and can be used to create very diverse music.

The natural minor originates from a type of scale used in early music called the **aeolian mode**. You will find that a lot of the plainchant we discussed in a previous unit uses the natural minor scale. In addition, when modern bands are playing in a minor key, they are frequently using this scale. Music that uses the natural minor scale typically has a sad, melancholy feel that might also be thought of as depressed, contemplative, or brooding.

The harmonic minor scale, however, is used in a lot of gypsy music. There is something about this scale that sound very passionate, and it fits well into the Spanish/**flamenco** lifestyle. This scale also sounds very Eastern, and many people relate it to Egyptian or Hungarian-style music. The harmonic minor scale can also sound angry, volatile, and unpredictable.

The most common minor scale used in classical music is the melodic minor scale. This is a very interesting scale because it starts off sounding sad, but at the end becomes happy like a major scale. It can't decide what it wants to be, almost as is it's bipolar. Even worse, when the scale descends, it goes back to being sad like the natural minor scale. Nonetheless, it is because of this variety and the melodic gestures it can produce that you will find this in a lot of traditional classical music.

9.6 Research and Discussion

The emotions we experience in life are not always black and white. As humans, we'll often feel many sensations at the same time, and feelings can change quickly from one minute to another. Music can be a refection of this as well. Not all music stays strictly within one emotional boundary – many songs and instrumentals can express as assortment of emotions within in the same piece of music.

- Find music that exemplifies the use of major and minor keys.

- What is this music about?

- What emotions are captured in the music?

- How do you relate to the music?

- What do you like or not like about the music?

9.7 Vocabulary

The following words pertaining to music were used in this unit. Look back through the chapter to find definitions and to make sure you understand them. An excellent online dictionary can be found at: http://www.music.vt.edu/musicdictionary

Relative key

Relative minor

Relative major

Courtesy accidental

Natural minor scale

Harmonic minor scale

Melodic minor scale

Aeolian mode

Flamenco

Unit 10

"Music is the wine
that fills the cup of silence."

~Robert Fripp

The music theory that we have learned, such as the scales and intervals, has to do with the melodic aspect of music. **Melody** is something that most people recognize when they hear it, but can be difficult to define. In simple terms, however, it's the part of the song that is most prominent, and usually the most recognizable. If you find yourself humming the tune of your favorite song, you're probably hooked on its melody.

Underneath the melody, however, there is a lot going on. This is called **harmony**. A good example of harmony is a piano or guitar accompanying a singer. Although the harmony is not often the first thing you notice, it is extremely important for it to be there. Different harmonies can, in fact, affect the way a melody sounds, and the quality of the music can greatly depend on a good harmony.

10.1 Theory

Chords and Triads

The basic element of harmony is called a **chord**. A chord is a set of notes grouped together in some way. Often the notes of a chord are played simultaneously, but they don't necessarily need to be. Since two pitches create an interval, chords are generally considered to be three or more notes.

To get more specific, a chord can be named based on how many notes are sounded. A five-note chord, for example would be a **pentachord**. A chord with three notes would be a **trichord**, a **hexachord** has six notes, etc. These kind of chords can be created with *any* set of notes – sometimes it will sound pretty, but it won't always.

Most of the music you hear – whether it's classical, country, or contemporary – is based on a specific kind of chord called a **triad**. These chords not only have three notes, but are based on the interval of a 3rd and always consist of a **root**, a **3rd**, and a **5th**.

The **root** of a triad is also the name of the triad. A **C triad** will have a root of C. When a triad is in **root position**, the root will always be the lowest note.

The next note of a triad (the 3rd) is found by going up a 3rd from the root.

The last note (the 5th) is found by going up another 3rd (This note is also a 5th up from the root).

You may notice a couple other things about the triad above. First, you are essentially writing every other note. Your first note was C, skip D, write E, skip F, write G. Because of this, the notes were all written on spaces. When a triad is in root position, the notes will either be on all spaces *or* all lines.

Here are some more examples of triads. Notice how they are written on all lines or all spaces, and all consist of a root, a 3rd, and a 5th.

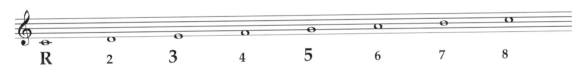

Major Triads

Just as there are different qualities of scales and intervals, there are different qualities of triads. A **major triad** is derived from the root, 3rd, and 5th of a major scale. To find a C major triad, look at the C major scale:

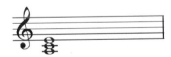

The notes of a C major triad are C (root), E (3rd), and G (5th).

When building major triads in this manner, be aware of accidentals within the scale. Try building a D major triad.

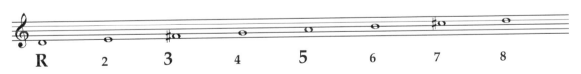

Because the third degree of the scale is F♯, a D major triad is D-F♯-A, not D-F-A. The latter is a triad, but not major.

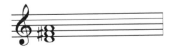

Try building more major triads.

Minor Triads

Once you are comfortable with major triads, finding other qualities is easy. A **minor triad** is created by lowering the 3rd of a major triad by a half step.

A minor triad doesn't require a flat. In the following example, lowering the 3rd (F♯) by a half step results in a natural note.

Here are more minor triads:

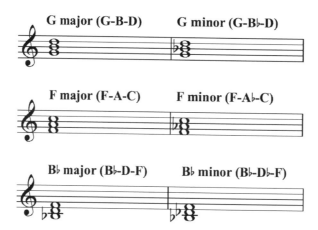

10.2 Rhythm

Fast 3/8 Time

Often times signatures that have a bottom note of 8 move at very quick tempos, and counting 1-2-3 1-2-3 very fast can get frustrating. In these cases, it facilitates things to count in larger groups. In 3/8, simply count a large group of "1."

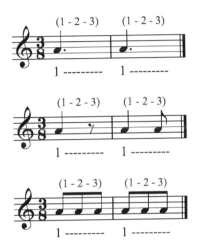

Fast 6/8 Time

6/8 at fast tempos can be problematic for the same reasons. Counting 1-2-3-4-5-6 quickly over and over can be exasperating. In this case, try counting two large groups.

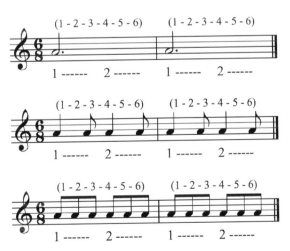

When you count in large groups like this, they are referred to as **compound meters**. To master this idea, practice clapping the exercises in your workbook.

10.3 Keyboard Skills

Now that we're working with harmony, we can incorporate some triads into the music we're playing. Take a look at the chords below. Most triads will use the same basic fingering.

Major Triads

Right Hand:

C Major:

G Major:

F Major:

Left Hand:

C Major:

G Major:

F Major:

Minor Triads

Right Hand:

A Minor:

E Minor:

D Minor:

<u>Left Hand:</u>

A Minor:

E Minor:

D Minor:

In your workbook, practice more exercises using triads.

10.4 Aural Skills

We're now going to practice recognizing major and minor triads. After all the other stuff we've done, this may actually be a bit easier. Just remember that major triads sound happy, and minor triads are sad. Take a look at the exercises in your workbook for extra practice.

10.5 Music Appreciation

The two most important parts of music are **melody** and **harmony**. Both are a little difficult to define, although they are the kind of things you "know when you hear them."

Melody refers to the most identifiable part of a piece of music. If you're singing along with a song in your car, you're usually singing the melody. The melody is a combination of notes and rhythm that is unique to that particular piece of music. Harmony can be thought of as the chords underneath a melody. Different harmonies can make the same melodic line sound very different.

There are many different ways to put melodies and harmonies together. In the case of a **singer-songwriter**, the performer would sing the melody, and the harmony would be the guitar or piano chords played along with them. If you have been part of a **choir**, you know there are **soprano**, **alto**, **tenor**, and **bass** voices. Usually the soprano has the melody and the other voices sing the harmonies. On piano, often times the right hand plays the melody, while the left hand takes care of the harmony.

Music that has both melody and harmony is called **homophonic** texture. By far the majority of music we hear consists of these two important elements. However, there are two other ways to describe **textures**:

Monophonic means "one sound" and refers to the fact that there is a single melody with no harmony underneath. Examples of this include one person singing alone, or many people all singing the exact same notes.

Polyphonic texture, or "many sounds," refers to many melodies happening at the same time. A common example of this is a **round**, which you probably remember singing when you were young. One person starts with "Row, row, row your boat," then someone else comes in with the same thing, then someone else, and so on and so forth. Everyone is singing a melody, but since they are all singing at different times it is polyphonic.

Textures such as these give music broader depth and capacity for expression. They are yet another tool musicians use to convey their art form.

10.6 Research and Discussion

Melodies, harmonies, and textures create a lot of variety in music. Find examples of music that is monophonic, homophonic, and polyphonic.

- How would you describe the texture of the music?

- Does the melody and harmony work well together?

- Do certain textures lend themselves to different kinds of music?

- Do you prefer one kind of texture to another?

- What are some ways that you hear melodies and harmonies being used in music?

- What different instruments create melody and harmony in music that you hear?

10.7 Vocabulary

The following words pertaining to music were used in this unit. Look back through the chapter to find definitions and to make sure you understand them. An excellent online dictionary can be found at: http://www.music.vt.edu/musicdictionary

Melody

Harmony

Chord

Trichord

Triad

Root

Major triad

Minor triad

Compound meter

Singer-songwriter

Choir

Soprano

Alto

Tenor

Bass

Texture

Homophonic

Monophonic

Polyphonic

Round

Unit 11

"The way to write American music is simple.
All you have to do is be an American
and then write any kind of music you wish."

~Virgil Thompson

Unit 11

Major and minor triads are two of the most common harmonies that you hear, but many other kinds of chords provide colorful variety. This unit will discuss two more possibilities based on the concept of triads that we learned in the previous chapter.

11.1 Theory

Augmented Triads

To find **augmented triads**, again start with the major. This time, raise the 5th by a half step. A C major triad (C-E-G) would become augmented by raising G to G♯.

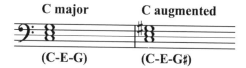

The only note that is altered is the 5th. The root and 3rd of the major triad remain the same, even if they include accidentals. D major (D-F♯-A) becomes D-F♯-A♯.

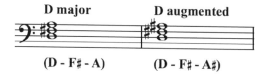

Here are some additional augmented triads:

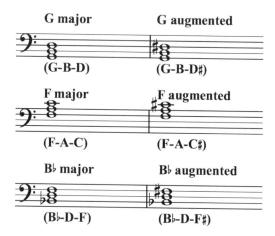

Diminished Triads

The final quality we will discuss is the **diminished triad**. To create this chord, lower the 3rd *and* 5th of a major triad by a half step. C major (C-E-G) becomes C-E♭-G♭.

When lowering a note that is already sharp, remember that it becomes natural. D major (D-F♯-A) becomes D-F♮-A♭.

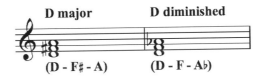

Here are some additional diminished triads:

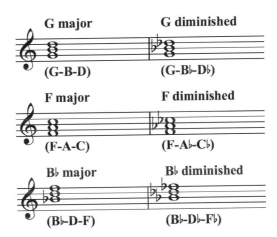

11.2 Rhythm

Rhythm Slashes

Often times jazz, rock, and pop music will not write out all the notes of a chord. Instead, they will write the name of the chord above the staff, and within the measure will be written **rhythm slashes**.

Rhythm slashes look similar to the rhythmic values we have already studied, but are slightly more angular.

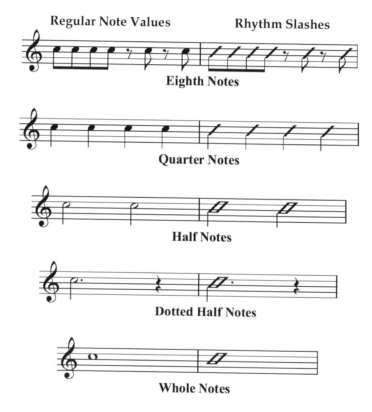

In these genres of music, chord names are often abbreviated or represented with symbols.

C or **CM**　　= C **major** triad

Cm or **Cmin** = C **minor** triad

Caug or **C+**　= C **augmented** triad

Cdim or **C°**　= C **diminished** triad

A score with rhythm slashes might look something like this:

11.3 Keyboard Skills

You already know major and minor triads on piano, so let's incorporate augmented and diminished chords. Below are fingerings for left and right hand harmonies.

Augmented Triads

Right Hand:

C Augmented:

G Augmented:

F Augmented:

147

Left Hand:

C Augmented:

G Augmented:

F Augmented:

Diminished Triads

Right Hand:

C Diminished:

G Diminished

F Diminished:

Left Hand:

C Diminished:

G Diminished:

F Diminished:

In your workbook, practice more exercises using triads.

11.4 Aural Skills

Recognizing augmented and diminished triads is much more difficult because they both sound unfamiliar to the ear. To practices identifying these, start first by choosing between minor and diminished, then major and augmented. As you get comfortable, try choosing between all four qualities. The exercises in your workbook will help you become adept at hearing these triads.

11.5 Music Appreciation

In the previous unit, we talked about 3/8 and 6/8 time signatures at fast tempos. These compound meters are used for many kinds of dances because of the active pace and rapid dynamic. **Waltzes**, for example, often use 3/8 time. If you listen to waltzes by Strauss or other classical composers, you will hear that the music correlates exactly with the 3/8 spirit. This is especially apparent when you can actually watch someone dancing to the music as well.

A lot of Irish music, such as the **jig**, is written in 6/8. The liveliness of the meter is a natural companion to the energetic dancing. The influence of Irish folk music is also found in American folk music; in fact, both countries claim many of the same tunes. One can hear a fiddler playing very similar melodies in the music of both traditions, and the singers are often telling the same stories.

11.6 Research and Discussion

Dance has been intertwined with music from almost the beginning of time. With very few exceptions, such as the liturgical music written exclusively to be sung in church during the Middle Ages, people have found ways to dance to music. Sometimes dancing can be formal: In the Renaissance, a lot of music was written for royalty, and even dances such as the waltz have specified steps. Other dances are more loosely structured, such as the **Lindy Hop** of the 1920s, the jigs and **reels** of Ireland, or even Country **line dancing** in America. Sometimes dancing just involves moving or swaying as you feel the music move you. However you react, dance and movement is an integral part of the musical experience.

- Find a piece of dance music.

- What style of music is this?

- What time signature is it in?

- What makes this good music to dance to?

- What kind of movement is required for the dancer?

- Who typically dances to this kind of music?

- Have you tried dancing to the music?

- What do you like or not like about this music/dance?

11.7 Vocabulary

The following words pertaining to music were used in this unit. Look back through the chapter to find definitions and to make sure you understand them. An excellent online dictionary can be found at: http://www.music.vt.edu/musicdictionary

Augmented triad

Diminished triad

Rhythm slash

Waltz

Jig

Lindy Hop

Reel

Line dancing

Unit 12

"It had never occurred to me before that music and thinking are so much alike. In fact you could say music is another way of thinking, or maybe thinking is another kind of music."

~ Ursula K. Le Guin

Unit 12

Triads are most useful when played in succession to create **chord progressions**. These patterns form the basis of the harmonic structure of songs, giving it form and shape. The ability to describe the parts of music is called **analysis**.

12.1 Theory

Harmonic Analysis

Triads can be built on any scale degree. When they are built using the notes from a certain scale, they are called **diatonic triads**. Another way of thinking of this concept is that all the chords must be played without alterations from the key signature.

The key of C major has no sharps or flats, so all the diatonic chords must be built with no accidentals. This means that all qualities of chords – major, minor, augmented, or diminished – are possible.

One way to identify, or analyze, these triads is by using Roman numerals. This kind of **harmonic analysis** is based on key signatures and major scales. The root triad is given the Roman numeral "I," the second "ii," and so on. Upper or lower case Roman numerals are used for different qualities of triads.

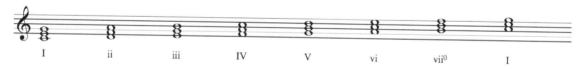

The last triad above is given the Roman numeral "I" (not "VIII") because it is the root triad and it does not matter where it appears on the staff.

Primary Triads

You may have heard people talk about the I, IV, and V chords of a key. These numbers refer to the harmonic analysis above. These three chords are known as the **primary triads** because they are the most important part of harmonic structure in much of the music you hear.

In major keys, these triads are always major. In the key of C major, the primary triads are C major, F major, and G major.

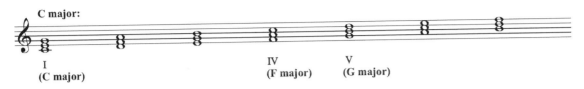

Note in the examples below that many of the chords contain accidentals, but the primary triads are always major.

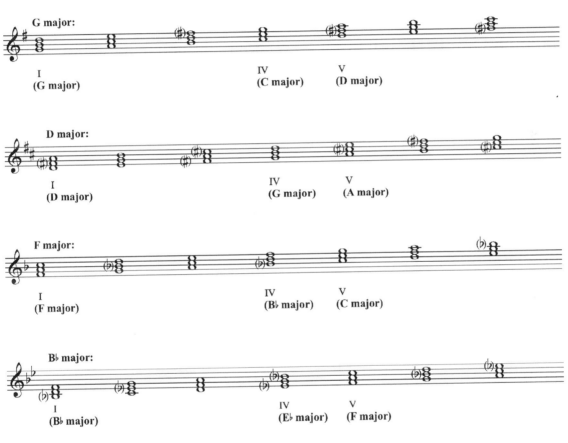

The Dominant 7th Chord

A 7th chord is not a chord with seven notes, but a triad that includes the interval of a seventh. 7th chords are created by adding one additional note on top of the existing three notes of a triad:

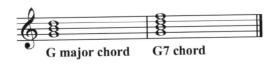

G major chord   G7 chord

155

There are many kinds of 7th chords, but the most common used in music is called a **dominant 7th**. This consists of a major triad with a minor 7th. If you look at the G7 chord above, you'll see that G-B-D creates a major triad, and G-F is a minor 7th. It is called a dominant 7th chord because it is built on the dominant scale degree. Using the Roman numerals above, this would be a V7 chord.

You can think of these chords as literally having two parts: 1) The dominant chord and 2) the 7th. In music, sometimes the V7 chord will be a substitute for the V chord.

Here are some additional examples. Note that some use accidentals to create the minor 7th.

12-Bar Blues

One genre of music that utilizes the primary triads frequently is **blues**. Many blues songs are written with a chord progression called the **12-bar blues** that consists of the I, IV, and V chords of a key.

This pattern starts off with four measures of I, followed by 2 bars of IV, then another 2 bars of I. The progression ends with one bar each of V, IV, I, and V again, making a total of 12 measures (or bars).

In the key of C major, the primary triads are C, F, and G major, so the 12-bar blues will look like this:

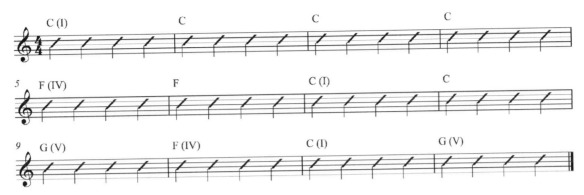

Usually this progression is repeated several times in a song, with different lyrics, melodies, or solos over top of it. When the performer is finally ready to end the song, they will usually play one last I chord.

This chord progression can be played in any key by substituting the primary triads. This is an important form to learn because it is the basis of many styles of music. The blues have inspired performers in folk, rock, punk, and many other genres.

12.2 Rhythm

Triplets

In addition to the familiar chord progression, the blues also have a very recognizable rhythm. In blues songs you often hear **triplets**. These are a group of three notes played in the amount of time it usually takes to play two of the same value. Triplets are identifiable by the "3" that appears above or below the group.

You can count triplets by saying "1-trip-let." Notice in the example below how they line up with the quarter note beat.

Swing 8ths

Almost all blues and jazz music is performed with **swing 8ths**. These rhythms differ from regular 8th notes because they sound a little "lazy."

Swing 8th notes look the same as standard 8th notes:

But are performed like a triplet missing the middle note:

Because swing 8ths look the same as regular eighth notes, you will often see
♪♪ = ♩♪ written at the beginning of a piece of music to indicate that it should "swing."

12.3 Keyboard Skills

So far, the lowest note of every triad has been the root note. When this happens, it is said to be in **root position**. In actual music, however, this will not always be the case – sometimes the 3rd or 5th will be the lowest note. Take a look at this chord:

The notes are E – G – C. If you take it at face value, it doesn't make sense as any kind of triad that we've learned. However, try rearranging the letters:

$$C - E - G$$

Now you can easily see that it's a C major triad. This is an important concept to understand: The notes C, E, and G always create a C major triad, no matter what order they are in.

When the 3rd of a triad is the lowest note (like the example above), it is said to be in **1st inversion**. Sometimes the 5th of a triad is the lowest note, like this:

This is called **2nd inversion**.

These upside-down triads can be used for a lot of different reasons. In piano music, you can use inversions to make smoother transitions from chord to chord. Take a look at the primary triads in the key of C:

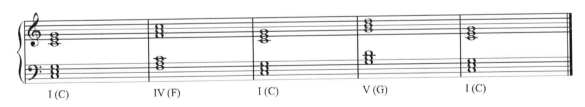

You can see that both hands have to jump around quite a bit to play this. Look how things change if you use inversions:

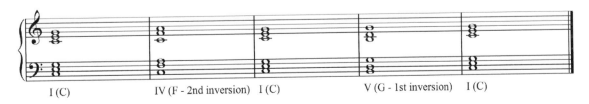

159

Now the hands don't need to move around so much. The chords are more connected, resulting in a smooth, uniform sound.

You can practice inversions more by looking at the exercises in your workbook.

12.4 Aural Skills

Throughout this book, we've talked about a lot of individual ideas regarding ear training. Let's start putting them together by combining rhythm, melody, and solfège. In these exercises, you'll be asked to identify which is the correct melody. Use the following process to help:

1. Write the solfège beneath the exercise and sing it so you know what it sounds like.

2. Listen to the audio example.

3. Compare it to the way you sang it and identify the one that matches what was played.

This is difficult to do at first, but with practice you will master it. Have fun!

12.5 Music Appreciation

Blues music is one of the richest parts of American music history. Originally played by African-Americans in the south, the music originated in the late 19th century. Like many folk art forms, the songs in these early days were not written, but learned and passed down by players from one generation to the next. Blues music wasn't published until 1912, and the first recording was in 1920, but even then many musicians could not read music and relied on oral history to pass on traditions.

The blues we hear today is much different from blues in the early 20th century. Not everyone may enjoy the sound of musicians such as **Lead Belly**, but it is indisputable that the blues have influenced almost all musical genres in some way. Blues became popularized in the 50s with performers such as **Elvis** and **Buddy Holly**, and many of the **Beatles** songs have a relationship with the blues. Even as electric guitars took over, heavy metal bands such as **Led Zeppelin** and **Black Sabbath** took influence from blues, sometimes covering old songs directly. The blues have continued to influence everything from **gospel, R&B,** and **rap** to **pop, punk,** and **country**. There are still many blues artists today, and it remains one of the most popular styles throughout the world.

12.6 Research and Discussion

Next to major scales, the primary triads are perhaps the most important concepts in music. We've already learned how they are used in the blues, but the truth is they are important to the structure of every genre. Sometimes this is done in an obvious way, other times it is much more subtle. To illustrate this, let's focus on the connection of the blues to modern music.

- Find a piece of modern music that is influenced by the blues.

- How does the blues influence this music?

- Can you hear similar chord progressions?

- If there are words, are there similarities in the vocal lines?

- How is this music different from the blues?

- Compare and contrast this music to a performance by an early blues musician, such as Lead Belly, Howlin' Wolf, or Muddy Waters.

- Which music do you like better? Why?

12.7 Vocabulary

The following words pertaining to music were used in this unit. Look back through the chapter to find definitions and to make sure you understand them. An excellent online dictionary can be found at: http://www.music.vt.edu/musicdictionary

Chord progressions

Harmonic analysis

Diatonic triads

Primary triads

Dominant 7th chord

12-bar blues

Triplet

Swing 8th

Root position

1st inversion

2nd inversion

Lead Belly

Elvis, Buddy Holly

The Beatles, Led Zeppelin, Black Sabbath

Gospel

R&B

Rap

Pop

Punk

Country

Unit 13

"Great music is that which penetrates the ear with
facility and leaves the memory with difficulty.
Magical music never leaves the memory."

~ Sir Thomas Beecham

Unit 13

Just as there are different kinds of literature (novels, poems, short stories, plays, essays etc.), there are different ways to write and organize music. These are called **forms**, and they help listeners make sense of music by utilizing patterns. You have already learned one form, the 12-bar blues. Although literally thousands of songs have been written using these same twelve measures, they are all unique and express the distinctive style of the composer. Just because music is written in a form does not mean it is unoriginal – think of how many novels have been written – on the contrary, a form is a device that allows the composer to express their original voice.

13.1 Theory

Binary Form

Musical forms are often described using letters to represent sections. The letter A, for example, might refer to one section of music, and the letter B would refer to a contrasting section with completely different music or words. You may use as many letters as you need for a piece of music, and if sections repeat you would use the same letter again.

Music that has two contrasting sections (**A B**) is called **binary form**. In songs, you might consider the A section the "verse" and the B section the "chorus." Even if these two parts repeat and nothing else is added, it would still be considered binary form.

In the Baroque Era, a dance called the **Minuet** was written in binary form. The most famous example of this is *Minuet in G*, a piece that was found in a collection of music titled *Notebook for Anna Magdalena Bach*, who was J. S. Bach's second wife. The music has been a staple of students learning piano for decades, and even if you don't recognize the name you have probably heard the music in a movie, TV show, or commercial. In the 1960s, a girl group called The Toys even recorded a doo-wop song based on the melody called *Lover's Concerto*.

Ternary Form

If the A section returns, (**A B A**), it would be considered **ternary** form. In this arrangement, there would be an opening section (**A**) followed by a section of completely different music (**B**). The original section (**A**) would then be performed again.

Rondo Form

If the A section is played many times with contrasting material in between, it is called a **rondo**. Here are some examples of how a rondo could be arranged::

A B A B A
A B A C A
A B A C A B A

Sometimes rondos can be arranged like palindromes, like in the last example above. A palindrome is a word or phrase that can be read the same both forward and backwards. Words like *bob* and *level* are two simple examples of this. Here are some more complicated palindromes:

- Poor Dan is in a droop.
- A man, a plan, a canal: Panama.
- Cigar? Toss it in a can. It is so tragic.
- Draw, O coward!
- Yo, bottoms up! (U.S. motto, boy.)

Canon

A **canon** is a complicated version of a **round**, which you may remember from elementary school. When singing a round, such as "Row, Row, Row Your Boat," one person begins singing the melody alone. A few bars later, someone else joins in singing the same melody, but at a different time. One by one, others join in. Everyone is singing the same thing, but at different times.

A canon is the same principle, but with more complicated music. The most famous example of this form is *Canon in D* by **Johann Pachelbel**, a piece frequently played at weddings and on concerts at Christmas time. One of the reasons this canon is so catchy is that is also employs something called a **ground bass**, which is a repeating bass line. Essentially, the same 8 chords repeat themselves throughout the entire piece while three instrument lines develop layer upon layer of beautiful melodic ideas.

In the early 2000s, a young guitarist who identified himself as funtwo uploaded a Youtube video that took the world by storm. It was a virtuosic rock version of Pachelbel's Canon on electric guitar, composed by another musician of internet fame, Jerry C, and complete with tapping, sweeping, and other flashy maneuvers. Although much of funtwo's version was entirely new, it was inspired by the Baroque master and introduced many young people to classical music.

Sonata

One of the most complicated forms of music is called **sonata form**. This form is found in a lot of classical and romantic music, and has been widely used by a variety of composers.

The first part of a sonata is called the **exposition**. It consists of the first musical themes and harmonies that will be found throughout the piece.

This is followed by a **development**. In this section, the music from the exposition is manipulated, new themes are introduced, and it passes through a number of different keys.

The third part is called the **recapitulation**, and is essentially the music from the exposition played again. However, it is often not played exactly as the beginning, but with some kind of variation.

The sonata usually ends with a **coda**, or a short passage of music that acts as a conclusion.

Although looking at the sections above may not sound difficult, it is made complicated because there are often sections within sections, the music changes keys within the same piece, and even repeated themes are sometime hard to identify because they are ornamented or changed. In spite of its complexity, or perhaps because of it, composers have turned to sonata form to give us some of the most important works in our musical heritage.

13.2 Rhythm

Dotted 8th Notes

The dot makes an appearance one more time. This time we're adding it to the 8th note.

= ¾ of a beat

(original note value) + (½ of original value)

The dotted 8th note is often used in conjunction with a 16th note. When this is the case, the two notes will be connected by a beam.

Dotted 8th notes should be counted in the way you would count 16th notes.

1 e&a 2 e&a 3 e&a 4e&a

These note values can be complicated, but add a lot of interesting variety to music.

Syncopation

Most music you hear or play emphasizes strong beats (the notes on the counts). When a weak beat is emphasized, it is called **syncopation**. In the example below, notice that there are accented quarter notes on the off beats.

1 & 2 & 3 & 4 &

Syncopation is found in all kinds of music, but it is especially prominent in styles such as big band, reggae, and ska. Practice the exercises in your workbook to become familiar with this concept.

13.3 Keyboard Skills

The piano exercises in this chapter will be putting together everything you're learned so far. You've certainly learned a lot, and you're on your way to becoming a great pianist. If you ever doubt yourself, just remember what Bach said: "It's easy to play any musical instrument: all you have to do is touch the right key at the right time and the instrument will play itself."

Good luck and enjoy!

13.4 Aural Skills

What we're about to do is the most difficult of anything we've done so far, but if you've been practicing the material in the previous chapters you'll be ready for it. In this unit you'll be asked to dictate (or write) the melodies you hear. As always, take it step by step:

1. Listen to the rhythm first. Write the rhythm you hear underneath the staff so you have it as a reference.

2. After you have the rhythm, fill in the notes. The first note is given to you, so use it as a reference. Listen for the intervals that we learned and use the song references to help you.

3. After you have filled in the rhythm and the notes, listen to it one last time to double check everything.

Don't be discouraged if you can't master this right away – this is one of the most difficult things to do when it comes to ear training. With practice, you will start to hear things more easily and be able to translate them to paper.

13.5 Music Appreciation

Many people use the word *song* to describe any piece of music, but technically a song is a piece of music specifically with words or lyrics. Some forms are found particularly often in songs.

Strophic means that the same melody repeats, but the words are different each time. Musically, you might analyze this form as **A A A** because the actual melody is repeating.

Through-composed means that no musical material is repeated at all. Words, melodies, and harmonies are completely new throughout the entire song and nothing repeats. This is found in a lot of music from the Middle Ages and the Renaissance, but not so much in modern popular music.

Another very common form is **A A B A** form. Many blues songs are written with this because it is essentially a simple form of the 12-bar blues. Most contemporary songs also follow a pattern of alternating **verse** and **chorus**, but songwriters will throw in a bridge, solo, or other twist to make it interesting.

Although the label of the **singer-songwriter** is a relatively recent description, the tradition itself goes back hundreds of years. In the Renaissance, a musician named **John Dowland** (1563-1626) become famous for the songs he wrote and performed on lute, and in the 19th century **Franz Schubert** (1797-1828) became known for his piano and voice music. The music was often performed in homes, where groups of friends would gather to socialize, much like coffee houses or bars today. Even the subject matter wasn't that different from today's writers – most of the lyrics were about love, lust, love-lost, and death. Dowland was so recognized for his melancholia that he even wrote a song titled "Always Dowland, Always Sad."

13.6 Research and Discussion

The forms and structures we've discussed in this unit are predominantly applied to classical music, but many of the terms can be applied to modern pop and rock genres as well. See if you can find music that is related to the expressions discussed in this chapter.

- Choose a piece of instrumental and/or vocal music.

- Using letters (A, B, C, etc.), how would you describe its form?

- Do any of the forms we discussed (binary, canon, etc.) apply to this piece of music?

- Compare and contrast this music with a piece of classical music.

- Find a song by John Dowland or Franz Schubert and read the words.

- What are the words about?

- Can you find a piece of modern music that deals with the same subject?

- What do you like (or not like) about this music?

13.7 Vocabulary

The following words pertaining to music were used in this unit. Look back through the chapter to find definitions and to make sure you understand them. An excellent online dictionary can be found at: http://www.music.vt.edu/musicdictionary

Form

Binary form

Minuet

Ternary form

Rondo

Palindrome

Canon

Round

Johann Pachelbel

Ground bass

Sonata

Exposition

Development

Recapitulation

Coda

Dotted eighth note

Syncopation

Strophic

Through-composed

John Dowland

Franz Schubert

I don't know anything about music.
In my line you don't have to."

~Elvis Presley

Assignments

Date:

_____

_____

_____

Date:

_____

_____

_____

Date:

_____

_____

_____

Date:

_____

_____

_____

Date:

_____

_____

_____

Date:

_____

_____

_____

Date:

_____

_____

_____

Date:

_____

_____

_____

Date:

_____

_____

_____

Date:

_____

_____

_____

Date:

_____

_____

Date:

_____

_____

_____

Date:

_____

_____

_____

Date:

_____

_____

_____

Date:

_____

_____

_____

Date:

_____

_____

_____

Date:

_____

_____

Date:

_____

_____

_____

Date:

_____

_____

_____

Date:

_____

_____

_____

Date:

_____

_____

_____

Date:

_____

_____

_____

Date:

_____

_____

About the Author

A musician of numerous passions, **J. Andrew Dickenson** is a performer, teacher, composer, conductor, administrator, writer, and arranger who has been showcased in a variety of prestigious locations around the world.

Founder of the Midnight Moon Ensemble with soprano Yeonjune Suh, Andrew has performed in some of the most celebrated venues in the United States (Carnegie Hall), Korea (KNUA Hall), and England (Penzance Guitar Festival). Andrew was an original founding member of both the New York Guitar Quartet and the guitar quartet 1 East, and has worked with high profile acts such as SONOS Chamber Orchestra and Trio Sorella. An avid protagonist of new music and art, Andrew actively commissions pioneering composers to write music for his performances, including Terry Champlin, Bryan Johanson, Brian Grundstrom, and Judah Adashi, Albert Carbonell Sauri, and Steven Stone. He has also collaborated with many multi-media artists to produce shows at Baltimore's *Augenmusik* festival, *Artscape*, the Maryland Institute of Art, and the Academy of Art in Philadelphia.

A scholarship winner from both the Peabody Conservatory of Music and the Mannes College of Music, Andrew's primary teachers include Julian Gray, Robert Trent, and Frederic Hand. He has also studied with Sergio Assad, Manuel Barrueco, Gilbert Biberian, Terry Champlin, Carlo Domeniconi, Peter Golladay, William Kanengiser, Michael Newman, and Laura Oltman.

Now a dedicated teacher himself, Andrew is an Assistant Professor of Music at Cecil College and former String Department Head at Concordia Conservatory. He is the author of the acclaimed *Guitar Fundamentals* series and has been published internationally in *Soundboard* and *Classical Guitar*. Andrew is also editor of NYlon Review, the newsletter of the New York City Classical Guitar Society, where he was President and Artistic Director for 4 years.

Andrew has recently been invited for several conducting engagements, and he is quickly becoming known for his precise directing, inventive programming, and his innovative arrangements. Arranging credits include *Carmen*, *West Side Story*, and *Man of La Mancha* for chamber orchestras as well as numerous pop and rock songs for classical ensembles. He has also written scores for various theater performances. His music can be heard on recordings by the Midnight Moon Ensemble.

GuitarFundamentals.com
MidnightMoonMusic.com